Bloom's

GUIDES

Beowulf

The Adventures of
 Huckleberry Finn
All the Pretty Horses
Animal Farm
The Autobiography of Malcolm X
The Awakening
Beloved
Beowulf
Brave New World
The Canterbury Tales
The Catcher in the Rye
The Chosen
The Crucible
Cry, the Beloved Country
Death of a Salesman
Fahrenheit 451
Frankenstein
The Glass Menagerie
The Grapes of Wrath
Great Expectations
The Great Gatsby
Hamlet
The Handmaid's Tale
The House on Mango Street
I Know Why the Caged Bird Sings
The Iliad
Invisible Man
Jane Eyre

Lord of the Flies
Macbeth
Maggie: A Girl of the Streets
The Member of the Wedding
The Metamorphosis
Native Son
1984
The Odyssey
Oedipus Rex
Of Mice and Men
One Hundred Years of Solitude
Pride and Prejudice
Ragtime
The Red Badge of Courage
Romeo and Juliet
The Scarlet Letter
A Separate Peace
Slaughterhouse-Five
Snow Falling on Cedars
The Stranger
A Streetcar Named Desire
The Sun Also Rises
A Tale of Two Cities
The Things They Carried
To Kill a Mockingbird
Uncle Tom's Cabin
The Waste Land
Wuthering Heights

Bloom's

GUIDES

Beowulf

Edited & with an Introduction
by Harold Bloom

BLOOM'S
LITERARY CRITICISM
An imprint of Infobase Publishing

Bloom's Guides: Beowulf

Copyright © 2008 by Infobase Publishing

Introduction © 2008 by Harold Bloom

Bloom's Literary Criticism
An imprint of Infobase Publishing
132 West 31st Street
New York, NY 10001

Library of Congress Cataloging-in-Publication Data
Beowulf / [edited by] Harold Bloom.
   p. cm. — (Bloom's guides)
   Includes bibliographical references and index.
   ISBN 978-0-7910-9432-7 (hardcover : acid-free paper) 1. Beowulf.
2. Epic poetry, English (Old)—History and criticism. I. Bloom, Harold.
   PR1585.B37 2008
   829'.3—dc22
                                              2007030234

Bloom's Literary Criticism books are available at special discounts when purchased in bulk quantities for businesses, associations, institutions, or sales promotions. Please call our Special Sales Department in New York at (212) 967-8800 or (800) 322-8755.

You can find Bloom's Literary Criticism on the World Wide Web at
http://www.chelseahouse.com

Contributing Editor: Alison Steinlau
Cover design by Takeshi Takahashi
Printed in the United States of America
Bang EJB 10 9 8 7 6 5 4 3 2 1
This book is printed on acid-free paper.

All links and Web addresses were checked and verified to be correct at the time of publication. Because of the dynamic nature of the Web, some addresses and links may have changed since publication and may no longer be valid.

Contents

Introduction

HAROLD BLOOM

The Old English epic *Beowulf* may have been written during the first half of the eighth century, or it may have been composed at about the year 1000, which is the date of the manuscript. Either way, it was written in a Christian Britain, but one with many memories of the pagan past. Is *Beowulf* a Christian poem? Just barely; in any case, it has a profoundly elegiac relation to its Germanic origins. Though the nameless poet of this heroic epic must have been at least ostensibly Christian, *Beowulf* eschews any mention of Jesus Christ, and all its biblical references are to the Old Testament. The prime human virtue exalted in the poem is courage; Beowulf fights primarily for fame, for the glory of becoming the prime Germanic hero, and secondarily he battles for gain, for treasure he can give away, so as to show his largess at bestowing gifts. Grendel and his even nastier mother are descendants of Cain, but they are not described as being enemies of Christ. Even the dragon of the poem's conclusion is by no means identified with the dragon of Revelation. Perhaps aesthetic tact governs the poet of *Beowulf*: his hero's virtues have nothing to do with salvation, and everything to do with warlike courage. When Beowulf's people, at the epic's conclusion, lament the death of their lord—"They said that among the world's kings, he was the mildest and gentlest of men, most kind to his people and most eager for praise"—mildness, gentleness, and kindness are hardly Christian, since they never are exercised toward Beowulf's human enemies, and that praise for which the hero was "most eager" is purely Germanic. Since the audience of *Beowulf* was definitely Christian, what were the motives of the poet?

One valid answer may be nostalgia, most brilliantly expressed by Ian Duncan:

As *Beowulf* progresses, the monumental records of past origins grow ambiguous and dark, from the bright mythic-heroic genealogies and creation songs of the opening, through the annals of ancient strife carved on the golden hilt from the Grendel hall, to the dragon hoard itself, a mysterious and sinister, possibly accursed relic, signifying racial extinctions. But Beowulf seems to recognize . . . that his affinity with the dragon has extended to a melancholy kinship. . . .

Hence the dark conclusion, where the dragon and the hero expire together. All of the poem then is a beautiful fading away of Germanic origins, presumably into the light of a Christian common day. An even subtler reading is offered by Fred C. Robinson, who sees the poem as a blend of pagan heroism and Christian regret. This double perspective does seem to be a prominent feature of *Beowulf* and reminds me of the double perspective of the *Aeneid*, a poem at once Augustan and Epicurean. But does *Beowulf* conclude with the triumph of the Christian vision? God's glory as a creator is extolled in the poem, but nowhere are we told of God's grace. Instead, there are tributes, despairing but firm, to fate, hardly a Christian power. Though the beliefs of the writer of *Beowulf* doubtless were Christian, his poetic sympathies pragmatically seem to reside in the heroic past.

The Story Behind the Story

Scholars consider the author of *Beowulf* an immensely gifted poet, but that is all that is really known about him. His name and biographical information were not preserved, leaving the issue open to much speculation. Some critics suggest that each of the poem's three fights may have been composed by a different author and later combined by others who added the various digressive narratives, but most subscribe to the notion of a single poet.

Judging from the poem's content and style, certain elements of *Beowulf*'s composition are clear. Whether or not the poet originally produced an oral or a written composition, the work definitely follows conventions of the oral poetic tradition. While the poet obviously had knowledge of Christianity, he also draws from traditional Germanic heroic poetry spread and passed down through minstrels. No character named Beowulf appears in any other known heroic poem, but his adventures slightly resemble those in the widely recounted "Bear's Son" tale (also called "Strong John" and "The Three Stolen Princesses"). Although *Beowulf* seems most connected to Old Norse folklore, some of it is based on fact; historical records document the existence of Hygelac, king of the Geats (and Beowulf's uncle in the story), who died in 521 C.E.

The only concrete evidence of the poet's existence is a *Beowulf* manuscript produced around 1000. Two different scribes copied the poet's work in West Saxon, an Old English literary dialect, and an early editor gave the poem its title. The only surviving copy, this manuscript was preserved in the library of Sir Robert Cotton and is currently housed in the manuscript codex Cotton Vitellius A. XV (collected with three prose stories about monsters and one poem fragment) in the British Museum. The manuscript was damaged by fire, but Icelandic scholar Grímur Thorkelin transcribed it and published an edition in 1815.

Since the early English masterpiece was first published, scholars have tried to determine where and when the work could have originated. They have employed the study of archaeology, history, linguistics, and Christianity in this pursuit but still have no conclusive answers. The poetic dialect does not indicate a specific time or region, nor does the representation of Christianity in the poem indicate a specific period. Historical knowledge can only narrow the date of composition to anywhere between the seventh century, closer to the time the Scandinavian leaders mentioned in the story actually lived, and the ninth century, when the Danes invaded England.

Within this broad time frame, there are a few likely places where the poet could have composed his work. In identifying areas of high culture and support for the arts, scholars have named two plausible candidates: the Anglo-Saxon kingdoms of Northumbria, in northern England, and Mercia, in south-central England. Northumbria seems a possible place of origin between 673 and 735, an era known as the age of Bede, after a noted teacher and historian. The court of King Aldfrith, who reigned from 685 to 705, welcomed scholars and poets.

During the reign of King Offa II (757–796), Mercia cultivated many learned artists, making it another likely home for the *Beowulf* poet. Offa was the most powerful English king of this time, and the digression in *Beowulf* mentioning Offa, king of Angeln in the fourth century, could have been meant as a tribute to a royal patron.

Seventh-century East Anglia, with the highly developed culture of the Wuffingas dynasty (625–55), has also been judged a possibility. Archaeologists unearthed a treasure burial at Sutton Hoo similar to the described burials of Scyld and Beowulf, and grave goods linked to royal burials in Uppsala, Sweden, have also been found that are similar to ones described in the poem. The Wuffingas dynasty and its first two kings, Wehha and Wuffa, who could have migrated from Uppsala to East Anglia, resemble the names Wylfingas, Weohstan, and Wiglaf mentioned in the poem. This mystery will never be solved, but the Beowulf poet lives on through the undisputed greatness of his work.

List of Characters

Beowulf, the hero of the poem, is an ideal warrior. Strong, brave, and always honorable and loyal to his kinsmen, he has an illustrious career, first as a warrior, then as a lord, then as king of the Geats. Beowulf's courage and skill help him vanquish Grendel, Grendel's mother, and the dragon, but this last victory costs him his life.

Grendel is a large monster who devours humans despite the fact that he somewhat resembles a man. He terrorizes Heorot, Hrothgar's mead hall in Denmark, for twelve years, killing anyone who spends the night in the hall. Grendel is protected against the threat of weapons but meets his match in Beowulf, who dismembers him with his powerful grip.

Grendel's mother, a smaller version of Grendel, attacks Heorot to avenge Grendel's death. Beowulf kills her with a magical ancient sword he finds in her lair.

Hrothgar, the king of the Scyldings or Danes, is a wise and generous ruler but is too old to protect his people from Grendel and Grendel's mother, a similar challenge Beowulf will face when he becomes an elder king. After Beowulf defeats the two monsters, Hrothgar gives him sage advice about the vicissitudes of life and the dangers of pride.

The dragon is a fire-breathing, snakelike monster that ultimately kills Beowulf, although it dies in the process. Unlike Grendel and his mother, the dragon is not particularly intelligent.

Unferth, a thane in Hrothgar's court, challenges Beowulf's accomplishments and is soundly chastised by him. Unferth eventually accepts Beowulf's superiority as a warrior and lends him his sword.

Wealhtheow, Hrothgar's wife, epitomizes the ideal queen in her generosity and hospitality toward thanes and guests. The hazards of her essentially diplomatic role are repeatedly expressed in tales of queens caught between warring peoples.

Hygelac is Beowulf's uncle and the king of the Geats. Like Hrothgar, he rewards Beowulf appropriately for his heroic actions.

Wiglaf is a young and inexperienced thane who is the only retainer to stand by Beowulf during his fight with the dragon. As befits an honorable thane, Wiglaf is willing to risk his life to repay his lord, who is also a kinsman, for all the gifts the younger man has received from him.

Summary and Analysis

Beowulf, the longest Anglo-Saxon poem in existence, is a deceptively simple tale about the adventures of a sixth-century Germanic hero who fights three monsters in what is now Denmark and Sweden. Beneath this straightforward and, to a modern reader, somewhat simplistic plot, however, lies a highly structured work filled with historical and legendary allusions that subtly parallel, contrast, and foreshadow the poem's action.

The work begins with the funeral of a great king, Scyld Scefing, the legendary founder of the Danish royal dynasty (**lines 1–63**). (It will end with the funeral of another great king— Beowulf, the poem's protagonist.) According to legend, Scyld was found alone in a boat laden with treasure when he was a child. Upon his death the Danes honor him by placing his body in another treasure ship and putting the ship out to sea.

Scyld Scefing's subjects begin to call themselves the Scyldings and are well ruled by his son Beowulf (usually referred to as Beow to differentiate him from the hero of the poem). Beow, in turn, is succeeded by his son Healfdene, who has four children: Heorogar, Hrothgar, Halga, and a daughter whose name has been lost but who married Onela, a Swedish (or in Anglo-Saxon terms, Scylfing) king.

Of these children, Hrothgar is especially successful in battle and becomes ruler of the Scyldings after Heorogar is killed (**lines 64–85**). Rulers at this time relied on the allegiance of warrior-retainers called thanes. Their relationship was embodied in the heroic code, which required of the thane unbounded courage in battle and absolute loyalty to the ruler. In exchange, a ruler was expected to protect and provide for his thanes (who, after all, could not support themselves if they were constantly away fighting). A ruler was supposed to share generously the wealth taken in conquest, giving lavish gifts to his thanes in reward for their services. In addition, he provided them with a mead hall—a place to live, with food, drink, and nightly entertainment.

The elderly Hrothgar is a good ruler and builds the largest and most lavish mead hall ever seen, calling it Heorot. Although the poet alludes to Heorot's later destruction during a war—the result of "the sharp-edged hate of [Hrothgar's] sworn son-in-law"—at this point it is a welcoming place where the king holds feasts and hands out treasure. *Beowulf* abounds with similar allusions to future sorrows embedded in a joyful present. These references to grim events to come, which the poet's original audience would readily recognize, serve one of the poem's primary themes: the vicissitudes of life and the impermanence of all human endeavors.

The noise and merriment of the festivities, particularly the song of a scop, or bard, praising God, proves a torment to one creature—Grendel, a powerful and evil monster who lives as an outcast on the nearby moors (**lines 86–193**). Grendel, the poem explains, is a descendant of the biblical character Cain, who killed his brother Abel and was cursed by God. All malevolent monsters are Cain's descendants; like Cain, they strive against God but ultimately in vain.

Enraged by the happy sounds coming from Heorot, Grendel waits for night to fall. Then he creeps into Heorot, seizes thirty sleeping thanes, and takes "his slaughtered feast of men to his lair." The next night, Grendel attacks again, until the frightened thanes abandon Heorot and sleep elsewhere.

For twelve years, Grendel terrorizes Heorot. Hrothgar is distraught at the deaths of his thanes, but the monster seems unappeasable. Although the Scyldings use Heorot during the day, at night Grendel takes up residence in the hall. Hrothgar and his men appeal to their heathen gods—a practice that *Beowulf*'s Christian author heartily condemns as ignorance of "God . . . our protector above, / the King of Glory"—but the "night-evil" continues.

Word of Grendel eventually reaches Beowulf, a thane of the Geat king Hygelac (**lines 194–370**). Strictly speaking, Grendel is no concern of the Geats, a group occupying what is today southern Sweden. But by risking his life in a dangerous battle, Beowulf can win honor (symbolized by the gold he could expect to be given by Hrothgar) and fame—which, it was believed, was the only thing that endured beyond this ephemeral life. Beowulf resolves to destroy the monster and, gathering fourteen fellow warriors, sets off by ship for Denmark. The ship is spotted by a Scylding watchman, who hurries down to the shore to find out who the approaching warriors are. Impressed by Beowulf's strong appearance and his explanation of why he and his men have come, the guard agrees to conduct the Geats to Heorot.

The well-armed Geats enter the mead hall and sit down on one of the hall's many benches. They excite considerable curiosity, and Hrothgar's herald, Wulfgar, asks them who they are. Beowulf tells him and asks to speak to Hrothgar. Wulfgar, also impressed by Beowulf's appearance, encourages his king to speak to them.

Hrothgar, it is determined, knew Beowulf's father, Ecgtheow, and has heard that Beowulf has "the strength of thirty [men] / in his mighty hand-grip." Hrothgar believes that God, "in the fullness of mercy," has sent Beowulf to deliver them from Grendel (**lines 371–490**). Although the author has revealed that these characters are not Christian, their religion—despite their earlier appeal to heathen gods—resembles the monotheism of the Old Testament Jews (rather than the actual religious beliefs of sixth-century Scandinavians).

Hrothgar agrees to speak with the Geats, and Beowulf introduces himself, reveals his mission, and gives an account of his previous exploits, including vanquishing a family of giants and slaughtering sea serpents. Asking Hrothgar's permission to fight Grendel, Beowulf says that, like the monster, he will forsake weapons and use only his bare hands. Expressing a decided fatalism, he declares, "Whoever death takes / will have to trust in the judgment of God." All he asks is that Hrothgar send his "war-shirt" to his king, Hygelac, should Grendel triumph. In agreeing to let Beowulf fight the monster, Hrothgar reveals that he harbored Beowulf's father after Ecgtheow had "struck up a mighty feud / . . . among the Wylfings" by killing a warrior named Heatholaf, and that Ecgtheow had sworn allegiance to him. Among Germanic warriors—as the poem's numerous accounts of blood feuds make clear—vengeance for the killing of a lord or kinsman was a moral imperative. Thus feuds created even more feuds, and a warrior without the protection of a lord was extremely vulnerable to acts of retribution.

The Geats and Scyldings sit down to feast before night falls (**lines 491–606**). A jealous Scylding, Unferth, "who would not grant that any other man / under the heavens might ever care more / for famous deeds than he himself," tries to shame Beowulf. He asks if Beowulf is the same warrior who once lost a seven-day swimming match to a man named Breca and declares that he expects similar failure if Beowulf challenges Grendel. Beowulf reveals that he and Breca did engage in a swimming match—in full armor, no less—but he did not lose. Rather, after five days at sea, Beowulf was attacked by sea monsters. He slaughtered all nine and came to shore in Finland—quite a swim from Sweden. Beowulf then chastises Unferth, declaring, "I never have heard / such struggle, sword-terror, told about you." He goes on to recriminate Unferth—and his fellow Scylding warriors—for their lack of courage and ferocity, which has brought shame to them and made Grendel's reign of terror possible:

> "I'll tell you a truth . . . :
> never would Grendel have done so much harm,
> the awesome monster, against your own leader,
> shameful in Heorot, if heart and intention,
> your great battle-spirit, were sharp as your words.
> But he has discovered he need not dread
> too great a feud, fierce rush of swords,
> not from your people, the 'Victory-Scyldings.'"

Tonight, Beowulf declares, he will show the monster "the courage and strength / of the Geats in combat."

The Scyldings are heartened by Beowulf's resolve (**lines 607–709**). Hrothgar's queen, Wealhtheow, comes forward and offers the mead cup to all the warriors, including Beowulf. Evening comes, and the Scyldings retire, leaving the Geats in the hall to face Grendel. Beowulf strips himself of his armor and weapons, and his retainers go to sleep fully expecting to be killed in the night. But God, the poet asserts, has granted the Geats "comfort and help, / a weaving of war-luck." Grendel glides into the hall, hoping to find a straggler or two (lines 710–836). Seeing a host of men, he exults in his luck, expecting to make a meal of them. Beowulf is quietly watching Grendel when the monster seizes and devours a nearby Geat. Grendel then reaches for Beowulf, who grabs the monster's arm in his mighty grip. Grendel quickly realizes that he is in trouble and attempts to escape, but the two engage in a tremendous fight that, the poem asserts, would have knocked down a lesser hall.

Beowulf's men try to hack the monster with their swords, but Grendel is charmed against "all weapons of battle." Grendel cannot shake Beowulf's grasp, however, and Beowulf rips off the monster's arm at the shoulder. Mortally wounded, Grendel flees Heorot, never to return. Beowulf is left with the greater glory—and Grendel's arm, complete from the shoulder to the clawlike fingers.

Morning comes, and the Scyldings are ecstatic to find that Grendel has been vanquished (lines 837–924). Some Scylding warriors follow the tracks of the wounded monster, who has returned to his den under a lake in the moors. Then they ride back to Heorot, speaking of Beowulf's tremendous deed. Along the way, a scop composes a poem celebrating Beowulf's victory, thus assuring that word of the hero's deeds will survive him. The scop goes on to tell the stories of the heroic Sigemund, who slew a dragon, and the tyrannical Heremod, who killed many of his own subjects before meeting his end. The Scyldings return to Heorot as Hrothgar enters.

Upon seeing Grendel's arm, Hrothgar thanks God and promises to love Beowulf as a son (lines 925–1062). Beowulf recounts the events of the night before, leaving the Scyldings, especially Unferth, appropriately impressed. A tremendous feast is held, during which Hrothgar gives Beowulf and the other Geats horses, armor, and treasure, including "the largest gold collar / ever heard of on earth." That gold collar links the present with the future as the poem reveals that the Geat king Hygelac will be wearing it when he dies in battle "that time he sought trouble, stirred up a feud, / a fight with the Frisians, in his pride and daring." The grisly battlefield and the joyous celebration in the mead hall are juxtaposed to great effect (". . . warriors rifled the corpses / after the battle-harvest. Dead Geats / filled the field. Now cheers for Beowulf rose"), again emphasizing the vicissitudes of men's fortunes.

During the celebration, a scop tells the tragic tale of a war between the Danes and the Jutes (**lines 1063–1250**). The account is especially sad because Hildeburh, the wife of the Jute king Finn was also the sister of the Danish king Hnaef. (Princesses often served as "peace-weavers"—they were given in marriage to rulers of other peoples as a way of settling conflicts.) But when war broke out between the two peoples, Hildeburh's brother and son fought on opposing sides, and both were killed. A short peace followed; then the new Danish king, Hengest, attacked the Jutes, killed Finn, and took Hildeburh back to Denmark.

After the scop has finished the tragic tale of one queen, another Danish queen, Wealhtheow, speaks of the unity of her people: "Each noble here is true to the other, / every kind heart death-loyal to lord." The irony is keen, for as the poet has implied, the treachery of Wealhtheow's nephew Hrothulf will eventually tear apart her family just as Hildeburh's family was destroyed.

The ominous tone is made more explicit as the thanes settle down in Heorot for the night (**lines 1251–1299**). One will be killed, the poet reports, because Grendel has a mother. As the thanes sleep, Grendel's mother comes to Heorot seeking revenge for the death of her son. Although not as strong or terrible as Grendel, she bursts into the hall and quickly kills a thane, escaping with his body—and with Grendel's arm.

Beowulf is spending the night elsewhere, but when morning comes he goes to Hrothgar's chambers and hears the bad news (**lines 1300–1382**). Hrothgar is distraught at the death of his thane, Aeschere, who was a trusted counselor. But he knows who committed the dastardly act: a female monster who had often been seen accompanying Grendel as he stalked the moors and whose lair is known to be under a lake not far from Heorot.

Hrothgar offers Beowulf more treasure if he will go to the lake and kill the monster.

Beowulf agrees (**lines 1383–1472**). In a speech that succinctly expresses the warrior's fatalistic outlook in the pursuit of renown, Beowulf declares,

> "Grieve not, wise king! Better it is
> for every man to avenge his friend
> than mourn overmuch. Each of us must come
> to the end of his life: let him who may
> win fame before death. That is the best
> memorial for a man after he is gone."

Hrothgar, Beowulf, and a group of warriors set out for the lake, which is a sinister place in the middle of a foreboding landscape. When they arrive, they see signs of the previous night's carnage: The water is red with blood, and Aeschere's head is lying nearby. The lake is also seething with serpents. A Geat bowman kills one with an arrow, and the others haul it ashore with their spears to reveal its gruesome, monstrous form.

Beowulf is nonetheless undaunted and gathers his armor, including a sword, Hrunting, lent to him by a repentant Unferth (**lines 1473–1590**). *Beowulf* contains many descriptions of famed swords and their histories. In this warrior culture, a well-made sword was more than a tool—it was a most prized possession, almost an object of veneration, and was passed down from generation to generation. Beowulf makes appropriate provisions for his treasure in case of his death and plunges into the water. Grendel's mother grabs him and pulls him toward her den, a cave at the bottom of the lake. Although protected by his armor, he cannot draw his sword and is beset by serpents. Once in the den, however, and free of the snake-infested lake, Beowulf seizes the initiative, striking Grendel's mother with Hrunting. But the blade does not "bite through to kill"—the first time, we are told, that "a word could be said against that great treasure."

Undaunted by Hrunting's failure, Beowulf, "battle-furious," grabs Grendel's mother by the shoulder and throws her to the floor. She quickly gets up, knocks him down, and sits on him, pulling out her knife to finish him off. But her blade cannot penetrate his armor, and Beowulf gets back onto his feet, at which point, the poet asserts, God decides the struggle in favor of good. Looking around, Beowulf spots a large ancient sword, "longer and heavier than any other man / could have carried in the play of war-strokes." He grabs this "shearer of life-threads," draws it, and strikes Grendel's mother. The sword slices through her neck, killing her. The cave is then illuminated by a light of mysterious origin, "even as from heaven comes the shining light / of God's candle." Using this light, Beowulf explores the den and finds Grendel's body, which he decapitates.

Meanwhile, the warriors standing around the lake see a tremendous amount of blood in the water and conclude that Beowulf has been killed (**lines 1591–1639**). The Scyldings return home, while the Geats maintain a mournful vigil. Beowulf, however, is experiencing even stranger events below. The blood from the monsters begins to melt the sword "in battle-bloody icicles" until Beowulf is left with only the jeweled hilt. Taking the hilt and Grendel's head, he leaves the den, rises to the surface of the lake, and swims ashore. His men are overjoyed to see him alive, and they return to Heorot, four of them carrying Grendel's oversized head on a spear.

At Heorot, Beowulf recounts his adventure and presents Hrothgar with the sword hilt (**lines 1640–1884**). The king praises Beowulf for his valor but urges him not to become like Heremod, who began his career as an illustrious warrior and ended it a parsimonious tyrant. In a sermonlike speech, Hrothgar declares that a hero that God permits to "travel far in delight"—that is, to enjoy happiness and pleasure for a long time—can easily assume that his good fortune will last forever. His "portion of arrogance / begins to increase," and, as he succumbs to the sins of pride and covetousness, "[h]is future state"—death—"is forgotten, forsworn, and so is God's favor." Hrothgar implores Beowulf to "guard against that awful curse . . . and choose the better, eternal gains." For though his "fame lives now," "sickness or war . . . or sword's swing / thrown spear, or hateful old age" will one day level Beowulf, just as he, Hrothgar, has been humbled by the twelve years of suffering and sorrow Grendel brought him. After Hrothgar's speech, a feast is served, and when night falls, the guests sleep peacefully in Heorot.

The next day Beowulf returns Hrunting to Unferth with thanks and takes his leave of Hrothgar. The two swear friendship, and Hrothgar gives Beowulf many gifts. With tears running down his face, the old king clasps Beowulf's neck and kisses him, expecting "that never again would they look on each other / as in this brave meeting." The Geats return to their ship, load their treasure, and set sail.

They quickly reach their lord's lands (lines 1885–1962). The poem praises their hall; their king, Hygelac; and especially their young and generous queen, Hygd, who is compared favorably with Modthrytho, a fourth-century queen who in her youth had any thane who looked at her face in the daytime put to death.

Beowulf and his men sit with Hygelac in his hall, and Beowulf recounts his adventures, praising Hrothgar's hospitality (lines 1963–2199). Beowulf also discusses the hostilities between Hrothgar's Danes and the Heathobards, a people from southern Denmark. Hrothgar is planning to have his daughter, Freawaru, marry the Heathobard prince Ingeld, in order to ensure peace between the two peoples. But Beowulf is not convinced that their enmity can be overcome by such a match. (His caution, as the poem's original audience would know, is justified. In 520 Ingeld attacked and burned Heorot before being routed by the Danes.)

Beowulf then brings in the treasure he was given by Hrothgar and presents it to Hygelac. In sharing his booty with his king—as in his conduct on the battlefield and in the mead hall—Beowulf shows himself to be a paragon of virtue, the poet maintains. He is "ever loyal" to Hygelac, his lord and kinsman, and generous toward Hygelac's queen, Hygd, giving her the gold necklace that Wealhtheow had bestowed on him. He has gained renown in battle but has "no savage mind"—he never kills "comrades in drink," reserving for its appropriate use on the battlefield "the gift / that God [has] given him, the greatest strength / that man ever had." Yet in his youth, the poet reveals, Beowulf had shown no signs of future greatness. The Geats "were convinced he was slow, or lazy, / a coward of a noble." As a result "he got little honor, / no gifts on the mead-bench from the lord of the [Geats]."

Now that he has proved his mettle, however, Beowulf receives ample reward from Hygelac, who gives him his father's gold-covered sword—the most prized among the Geats—as well as land, a hall, and a throne of his own. Beowulf is now a lord.

Several years pass, and Hygelac is killed in battle (**lines 2200–2277**). His son, Heardred, is also killed, and the kingdom passes to Beowulf. Beowulf's rule is a prosperous time that lasts fifty years, until a fugitive stumbles into a vaulted barrow filled with treasure and—while its guardian, a dragon, sleeps—makes off with a precious cup.

Under the dragon's watchful eye, the hoard—the combined wealth of a people destroyed by war—had been undisturbed for three hundred years (**lines 2278–2311**). But now, as the fugitive brings the cup back to his lord as a peace offering, the dragon awakes, sees the intruder's footprints, and, checking his treasure, realizes that he has been robbed.

Though the dragon (who is not presented as a particularly intelligent creature) has no idea what the treasure is and certainly cannot use it, the theft angers him. That night he seeks retribution, burning houses, including Beowulf's hall, the "gift-throne of the Geats" (**lines 2312–2344**). To Beowulf, this causes "great anguish, pain deep in mind"—in large part because he fears that it might be divine punishment for some sin he has committed. Though filled "with dark thoughts strange to his mind," he promptly readies himself to battle the beast. Realizing that the traditional wood shield will be of little use against the dragon's flames, he orders a special shield of iron made. This will not be enough to save him, for, as the poet reveals, Beowulf is destined "to reach the end of his sea-faring days, / his life in this world, together with the serpent."

As in Beowulf's younger days, when he singlehandedly fought Grendel and Grendel's mother, the old ruler scorns the notion of approaching his enemy "with troops, with a full army"; having "endured / much violence before, taken great risks / in the smash of battles," he does not fear the dragon.

At this point, the poem reflects upon the highlights of Beowulf's illustrious career before he became king (**lines 2345–2509**). After the battle in which Hygelac was killed (which took place in Frisia, in what is now the Netherlands), Beowulf swam back to southern Sweden, carrying as trophies the armor of no less than thirty warriors he had slain. He so impressed Hygd that she offered him the throne over her own son, Heardred. The ever-noble Beowulf turned her down, however, and supported Heardred "among his people with friendly wisdom, / kept him in honor, until he grew older, / [and] could rule the Geats." When a usurper, Onela, seized the Scylfing throne and exiled the rightful heirs—Eanmund and Eadgils—Heardred gave them refuge, and Onela attacked his hall and killed Heardred and Eanmund in retaliation. Beowulf then became the Geat king and supported Eadgils in his successful attempt to retake the Scylfing throne.

"And so he survived," the poet says, "every encounter, every awful conflict, / heroic battles, till that one day / when he had to fight against the worm [dragon]." Having heard how the feud with the dragon began, Beowulf sets out for the dragon's lair with eleven retainers, guided reluctantly by the fugitive who had stolen the cup (**lines 2510–2601**).

When they reach the lair, Beowulf, his spirit "sad, / restless, death-ripe," speaks to his men of events important to his life and to the history of the Geat people. Central to this speech are the concepts of vengeance and honor. Beowulf recounts the story of how Haethcyn, his uncle, accidentally killed his own brother Herebeald—an act made all the more horrible because it could not be avenged, as that would involve murdering a kinsman. Brokenhearted, Hrethel—who was Haethcyn and Herebeald's father as well as the king of the Geats—died, and the Scylfings seized the opportunity to attack the Geats (an event that will presumably happen again after Beowulf's death). "My kinsmen and leaders avenged that well," Beowulf says, though in the battle Haethcyn, who had assumed the Geat throne, was killed. The next day "the third brother," Hygelac, "brought full vengeance / back to the slayer" when Ongentheow, the Scylfing king, was killed. Beowulf then touches on the exploits he performed in service to Hygelac, including his slaying of the champion of an enemy people, the Hugas, with his bare hands. "I wish even now," he declares, "to seek a quarrel, do a great deed."

He insists on fighting the dragon alone and commands his men to wait nearby. Although this demonstrates that Beowulf has not lost his valor or desire for renown, some commentators view it as an essentially irresponsible act, an example of the kind of pride Hrothgar had warned him against years before. For Beowulf's death, which might have been unnecessary, will bring calamity to his people.

When Beowulf heads to the entrance of the dragon's lair with a shout to announce his presence, the dragon comes out breathing flames. Beowulf's armor protects him from the fire, but when he strikes the beast, his sword fails him and the dragon is only slightly wounded. The two rush together again, and Beowulf is hurt.

In the meantime, Beowulf's men have deserted him and run off into the woods. One, however, a young man named Wiglaf, who is a kinsman of Beowulf's, remembers the favors the king has shown them and implores his comrades to come to Beowulf's aid (**lines 2602–2705**). No one responds, so Wiglaf alone takes up his sword (an old family heirloom) in Beowulf's defense—the first time the young retainer has fought for his lord. As Wiglaf joins Beowulf, the dragon charges again and burns up the thane's wooden shield. Wiglaf takes refuge behind Beowulf's shield while Beowulf strikes the dragon with all his strength—only to have his sword shatter on the dragon's skull.

The dragon charges again, biting Beowulf with his huge teeth and burning him with his fire. Wiglaf proves resolute, and despite the flames, he strikes the dragon. His blow lessens the dragon's fire, giving Beowulf the chance to pull out his knife and deliver the killing stroke to the dragon's belly.

The dragon is vanquished, but Beowulf has been fatally wounded, for the dragon's bite is poisonous (**lines 2706–2820**). Wiglaf washes Beowulf's wounds, and the king, recognizing that he will soon die, laments the fact that he has no son to take his place. He professes joy in his fifty-year reign, however, for during this time no foreign ruler had dared to "seek out a battle, / make any onslaught, terror, oppression, / upon Geatish men." Nor had Beowulf sought any intrigue, sworn deceitful oaths, or harmed his kin. Just as he had previously been an ideal thane, Beowulf, it seems, has been an ideal ruler.

Beowulf now directs Wiglaf to bring out some of the dragon's treasure—so that he "may more easily give up [his] life / and the dear kingdom that [he has] ruled long." Wiglaf obeys, but by the time he returns, Beowulf has lost consciousness. Wiglaf revives him with some water, and Beowulf, seeing the treasure, declares,

> "I give thanks aloud to the Lord of all,
> King of Glories, eternal Ruler,
> for the bright treasures I can see here,
> that I might have gained such gifts as these
> for the sake of my people before I died."

With his last breaths, he directs Wiglaf "to watch / the country's needs" and gives instructions for his funeral and for the creation of a large barrow on a cliff to serve as his memorial. Then he gives Wiglaf (who is the last of the Waegmundings, a family to which Beowulf also belongs) his gold necklace, helmet, rings, and mail-shirt. After observing that fate has swept away all his noble kinsmen and he must follow, Beowulf dies.

Wiglaf is saddened by his lord's death, although the poem points out that Beowulf performed an important service to his people by killing the dragon (**lines 2821–3027**). Wiglaf returns to the cowardly retainers, accusing them of desertion and predicting that their ignominy will haunt them for the rest of their lives. He then sends a messenger to relay to the Geats news of Beowulf's death. The messenger does so, predicting that their enemies—especially the Scylfings—will attack them now that their protector is gone and summarizing the feud between the Geats and Scylfings. The Geats gather to see Beowulf and the dragon, whose treasure is revealed to have been cursed (**lines 3028–3182**). Wiglaf leads some of the Geats into the dragon's cave, where they gather treasure to bury with Beowulf. They then push the dragon's body into the sea. Beowulf's people bury the remains from his funeral pyre, along with all the treasure, in the memorial barrow they construct. They bemoan the loss of their leader, who was "of the kings in this world, / the kindest to his men, the most courteous man, / the best to his people, and the most eager for fame."

(In Old English poetry, each line was divided into two halves, which were separated by a pause, or caesura. For the sake of typographical simplicity, the caesura has not been rendered here. All quotations are from Howell D. Chickering Jr.'s 1977 translation.)

Critical Views

J.R.R. Tolkien on Poetic Structure

The general structure of the poem, so viewed, is not really difficult to perceive, if we look to the main points, the strategy, and neglect the many points of minor tactics. We must dismiss, of course, from mind the notion that *Beowulf* is a 'narrative poem', that it tells a tale or intends to tell a tale sequentially. The poem 'lacks steady advance': so Klaeber heads a critical section in his edition.[27] But the poem was not meant to advance, steadily or unsteadily. It is essentially a balance, an opposition of ends and beginnings. In its simplest terms it is a contrasted description of two moments in a great life, rising and setting; an elaboration of the ancient and intensely moving contrast between youth and age, first achievement and final death. It is divided in consequence into two opposed portions, different in matter, manner, and length: A from 1 to 2199 (including an exordium of 52 lines); B from 2200 to 3182 (the end). There is no reason to cavil at this proportion; in any case, for the purpose and the production of the required effect, it proves in practice to be right.

This simple and *static* structure, solid and strong, is in each part much diversified, and capable of enduring this treatment. In the conduct of the presentation of Beowulf's rise to fame on the one hand, and of his kingship and death on the other, criticism can find things to question, especially if it is captious, but also much to praise, if it is attentive. But the only serious weakness, or apparent weakness, is the long recapitulation: the report of Beowulf to Hygelac. This recapitulation is well done. Without serious discrepancy[28] it retells rapidly the events in Heorot, and retouches the account; and it serves to illustrate, since he himself describes his own deeds, yet more vividly the character of a young man, singled out by destiny, as he steps suddenly forth in his full powers. Yet this is perhaps not quite sufficient to justify the repetition. The explanation, if not complete justification, is probably to be sought in different directions.

For one thing, the old tale was not first told or invented by this poet. So much is clear from investigation of the folk-tale analogues. Even the legendary association of the Scylding court with a marauding monster, and with the arrival from abroad of a champion and deliverer was probably already old. The plot was not the poet's; and though he has infused feeling and significance into its crude material, that plot was not a perfect vehicle of the theme or themes that came to hidden life in the poet's mind as he worked upon it. Not an unusual event in literature. For the contrast—youth and death—it would probably have been better, if we had no journeying. If the single nation of the *Geatas* had been the scene, we should have felt the stage not narrower, but symbolically wider. More plainly should we have perceived in one people and their hero all mankind and its heroes. This at any rate I have always myself felt in reading *Beowulf*; but I have also felt that this defect is rectified by the bringing of the tale of Grendel to Geatland. As Beowulf stands in Hygelac's hail and tells his story, he sets his feet firm again in the land of his own people, and is no longer in danger of appearing a mere *wrecca*, an errant adventurer and slayer of bogies that do not concern him.

There is in fact a double division in the poem: the fundamental one already referred to, and a secondary but important division at line 1887. After that the essentials of the previous part are taken up and compacted, so that all the tragedy of Beowulf is contained between 1888 and the end.[29] But, of course, without the first half we should miss much incidental illustration; we should miss also the dark background of the court of Heorot that loomed as large in glory and doom in ancient northern imagination as the court of Arthur: no vision of the past was complete without it. And (most important) we should lose the direct contrast of youth and age in the persons of Beowulf and Hrothgar which is one of the chief purposes of this section: it ends with the pregnant words *oþ þæt hine yldo benam mægenes wynnum, se þe oft manegum scod.*

In any case we must not view this poem as in intention an exciting narrative or a romantic tale. The very nature of Old English metre is often misjudged. In it there is no single rhythmic pattern progressing from the beginning of a line to the end, and repeated with variation in other lines: The lines do not go according to a tune. They are founded on a balance; an opposition between two halves of roughly equivalent[30] phonetic weight, and significant content, which are more often rhythmically contrasted than similar. They are more like masonry than music. In this fundamental fact of poetic expression I think there is a parallel to the total structure of *Beowulf*. *Beowulf* is indeed the most successful Old English poem because in it the elements, language, metre, theme, structure, are all most nearly in harmony. Judgement of the verse has often gone astray through listening for an accentual rhythm and pattern: and it seems to halt and stumble. Judgement of the theme goes astray through considering it as the narrative handling of a plot: and it seems to halt and stumble. Language and verse, of course, differ from stone or wood or paint, and can be only heard or read in a time-sequence; so that in any poem that deals at all with characters and events some narrative element must be present. We have none the less in *Beowulf* a method and structure that within the limits of the verse-kind approaches rather to sculpture or painting. It is a composition not a tune.

This is clear in the second half. In the struggle with Grendel one can as a reader dismiss the certainty of literary experience that the hero will not in fact perish, and allow oneself to share the hopes and fears of the Geats upon the shore. In the second part the author has no desire whatever that the issue should remain open, even according to literary convention. There is no need to hasten like the messenger, who rode to bear the lamentable news to the waiting people (2892 ff.). They may have hoped, but we are not supposed to. By now we are supposed to have grasped the plan. Disaster is foreboded. Defeat is the theme. Triumph over the foes of man's precarious fortress is over, and we approach slowly and reluctantly the inevitable victory of death.[31]

'In structure', it was said of *Beowulf*, 'it is curiously weak, in a sense preposterous,' though great merits of detail were allowed. In structure actually it is curiously strong, in a sense inevitable, though there are defects of detail. The general design of the poet is not only defensible, it is, I think, admirable. There may have previously existed stirring verse dealing in straightforward manner and even in natural sequence with Beowulf's deeds, or with the fall of Hygelac; or again with the fluctuations of the feud between the houses of Hrethel the Geat and Ongentheow the Swede; or with the tragedy of the Heathobards, and the treason that destroyed the Scylding dynasty. Indeed this must be admitted to be practically certain: it was the existence of such connected legends—connected in the mind, not necessarily dealt with in chronicle fashion or in long semi-historical poems—that permitted the peculiar use of them in *Beowulf*. This poem cannot be criticized or comprehended, if its original audience is imagined in like case to ourselves, possessing only *Beowulf* in splendid isolation. For *Beowulf* was not designed to tell the tale of Hygelac's fall, or for that matter to give the whole biography of Beowulf, still less to write the history of the Geatish kingdom and its downfall. But it used knowledge of these things for its own purpose—to give that sense of perspective, of antiquity with a greater and yet darker antiquity behind. These things are mainly on the outer edges or in the background because they belong there, if they are to function in this way. But in the centre we have an heroic figure of enlarged proportions.

Beowulf is not an 'epic', not even a magnified 'lay'. No terms borrowed from Greek or other literatures exactly fit: there is no reason why they should. Though if we must have a term, we should choose rather 'elegy'. It is an heroic-elegiac poem; and in a sense all its first 3,136 lines are the prelude to a dirge: *him þa gegiredan Geata leode ad ofer eorðan unwaclicne*: one of the most moving ever written. But for the universal significance which is given to the fortunes of its hero it is an enhancement and not a detraction, in fact it is necessary, that his final foe should be not some Swedish prince, or treacherous friend, but a dragon: a thing made by imagination for just such a purpose. Nowhere does a dragon come in so precisely where he should. But if the hero falls before a dragon, then certainly he should achieve his early glory by vanquishing a foe of similar order.

There is, I think, no criticism more beside the mark than that which some have made, complaining that it is monsters in both halves that is so disgusting; one they could have stomached more easily. That is nonsense. I can see the point of asking for *no* monsters. I can also see the point of the situation in *Beowulf*. But no point at all in mere reduction of numbers. It would really have been preposterous, if the poet had recounted Beowulf's rise to fame in a 'typical' or 'commonplace' war in Frisia, and then ended him with a dragon. Or if he had told of his cleansing of Heorot, and then brought him to defeat and death in a 'wild' or 'trivial' Swedish invasion! If the dragon is the right end for Beowulf, and I agree with the author that it is, then Grendel is an eminently suitable beginning. They are creatures, *feond mancynnes*, of a similar order and kindred significance. Triumph over the lesser and more nearly human is cancelled by defeat before the older and more elemental. And the conquest of the ogres comes at the right moment: not in earliest youth, though the nicors are referred to in Beowulf's *geogoðfeore* as a presage of the kind of hero we have to deal with; and not during the later period of recognized ability and prowess;[32] but in that first moment, which often comes in great lives, when men look up in surprise and see that a hero has unawares leaped forth. The placing of the dragon is inevitable: a man can but die upon his death-day.

Notes

27. Though only explicitly referred to here and in disagreement, this edition is, of course, of great authority, and all who have used it have learned much from it.

28. I am not concerned with minor discrepancies at any point in the poem. They are no proof of composite authorship, nor even of incompetent authorship. It is very difficult, even in a newly invented tale of any length, to avoid such defects; more so still in rehandling old and oft-told tales. The points that are seized in the study, with a copy that can be indexed and turned to and fro (even if never read straight through as it was meant to be), are usually such as may easily escape an author and still more easily his natural audience. Virgil certainly does not escape such faults, even within the limits of a single book. Modern printed tales, that have presumably had the advantage

of proof-correction, can even be observed to hesitate in the heroine's Christian name.

29. The least satisfactory arrangement possible is thus to read only lines 1–1887 and not the remainder. This procedure has none the less been, from time to time, directed or encouraged by more than one 'English syllabus'.

30. Equivalent, but not necessarily *equal*, certainly not as such things may be measured by machines.

31. That the particular bearer of enmity, the Dragon, also dies is important chiefly to Beowulf himself. He was a great man. Not many even in dying can achieve the death of a single worm, or the temporary salvation of their kindred. Within the limits of human life Beowulf neither lived nor died in vain—brave men might say. But there is no hint, indeed there are many to the contrary, that it was a war to end war, or a dragon-fight to end dragons. It is the end of Beowulf, and of the hope of his people.

32. We do, however, learn incidentally much of this period: it is not strictly true, even of our poem as it is, to say that after the deeds in Heorot Beowulf 'has nothing else to do'. Great heroes, like great saints, should show themselves capable of dealing also with the ordinary things of life, even though they may do so with a strength more than ordinary. We may wish to be assured of this (and the poet has assured us), without demanding that he should put such things in the centre, when they are not the centre of his thought.

JOAN BLOMFIELD ON STYLE

The setting out of the material is not in *Beowulf* an evolution, following one main line or connecting thread. Instead, the subject is disposed as a circumscribed field in which the themes are drawn out by a centre of attraction—in this case, the character of the good warrior. Far-flung tales and allusions, apparently scattered material and disconnected events are grouped in a wide sweep around the hero's character. In fact, these *are* his character, and their significance in the poem consists in this particular relation; by comparisons we are shown Beowulf's nature, by searchlights into the past and future we are to sense the magnitude and true import of his achievements. From this periphery he draws his substance and reality. By these means he lives and his destiny impregnates the whole poem. The good warrior is displayed as a being consummated

32

through all phases of his life and in all aspects of his character. The whole progress from adventurous youth to wisdom-weighted old age, many discreet elements—the bear-warrior strength, the knightly courtesy, vanity beside humility, and so on—are comprehended in this static unity. It has often been observed that there is no development of plot or character. The concluding state of affairs must be implicit in the beginning. With such a plan, a pre-ordained course of events, familiar topics, and stock situations are essential for the achievement of depth and scope. Not by transitions and transformations but by suggestion of the ever-present identity of seed in fruit and fruit in seed does the poet adjust the emotional tension. The reference to the burning of Heorot woven into the description of its first glories, and the forecast of family strife while yet all is well in Hroðgar's court are straightforward instances. More complex is the messenger's announcement of Beowulf's death[1]: at great length he recounts the rising to power of the Geats—now to fall a prey to peoples they had overcome; their downfall will be the direct consequence of Beowulf's death—who died in defending them; he *þe us beagas geaf* has gained with his last breath yet more *beagas*,[2] treasure which is thus his personal perquisite, which in perishing with him on the pyre, shall symbolize the joys now to pass for ever from the Geats.[3] This tendency to antithesis, frequently verging on paradox, and the constant play of irony are but stylistic manifestations of those movements of the poet's thought which shape the very stuff of the poem.

Stylistic detail might be expected to give reliable indications of the lines on which the theme is constructed; and it is fortunate that the style of Beowulf has attracted a large share of the most discerning criticism. Analysis of style is in this case a justifiable approach to analysis of structure. The general impression that *Beowulf*, lacking clarity and speed, is remarkable rather for depth and vibrancy needs explanation in terms both of style and of structure. These effects are partly due to a method of evocation and cross-reference in which contrast is an important element. Notable examples of description by contrast are the allusions to Sigemund, Heremod, and Offa; and there are constant lesser instances of this method and its corollary, parallelism. As a structural principle, it may be traced in the antiphonal exordium. We hear first of the mighty destiny and wide fame of the Scyldings.[4] The crescendo of Scylding power rouses opposing forces of cunning evil ever lurking to reverse the prosperity of mankind; by Grendel's raids the fame of the Scyldings is blasted, the utmost human effort frustrated, the mightiest of rulers made impotent. Beowulf is then introduced in the all-powerful enterprise of untried youth. Here the concentration of the double flow increases: for Beowulf is connected with Hroðgar both by grateful allegiance, because of the favour shown to his father, and by his undertaking the trial of valour where others have failed. Complementing the knowledge that Hroðgar his *hold wine* is in need is Beowulf's desire to crown his exploits by the supreme enterprise of *ðing wið þyrse*. The duty of allegiance emerges in Hroðgar's recapitulation of Beowulf's *æþelu* (457–72), the demands of Beowulf's career in his own account of his setting forth[5] (405–41). Both are presaged in the greeting of Wulfgar (338–9), who recognizes in the bearing of Beowulf the *wlenco* and *higeþrymm* which have brought him to Heorot, as contrasted with *wræcsið* (which brought his father). The allusion is oblique—Wulfgar is challenging Beowulf as a stranger—and its application by so much the more pointed. This same alternation is at work throughout the poem. The suspension of the theme—the "balance" of which Professor Tolkien speaks—demands a constant confrontation of similar and dissimilar.

A fundamental element in this balance is the poet's distribution of his material within the orbit of a central idea. The descriptive method of recurrence-with-elaboration distributes epithets and qualifying phrases in this way. The simplest form is piling of varied repetition, of the type: *eorlscipe efnde, ealdre geneðde, mare o fremede* (2,132–3).[6] More complicated is the type: *þonne heoru bunden, hamere geþruen, sweord swate fah swin ofer helme ecgum dyhtig andweard scireð* (128–7), or *forðon he ær fela nearo neðende niða gedigde, hildehlemma, syððan he Hroðgares, sigoreadig seeg, sele fælsode; and at guðe forgrap Grendeles mægum Wan cynnes* (2,349–53).[7]

Here the amplification of several interdependent ideas is carried through by turns, so that the parts of the sentence are interlocked by a spaced and cumulative reinforcement—a method which reaches its ultimate development in the poetry of the Norse skalds. And in the last analysis, the "synonyms" so characteristic of Old English poetic diction express in little the multiplicity, the resolution into separate aspects, shown in the presentation of the theme itself.

For the structure of the poem is not sequential, but complemental; at the outset certain parts of a situation are displayed, and these are given coherence and significance by progressive addition of its other parts. Already Klaeber has noticed a circumscribing movement, and in the most penetrating passages of his criticism he constantly recurs to this idea.[8] He recognizes "an organic relation between the rhetorical characteristics and certain narrower linguistic facts as well as the broader stylistic features and peculiarities of the narrative" (p. lxv), citing in particular "retardation by means of variations and parenthetical utterances" and further elaborating the idea in his statement: "The preponderance of the nominal over the verbal element, one of the outstanding features of the ancient diction, runs parallel to the favourite practice of stating merely the result of an action and of dwelling on a state or situation." Yet having worked out this organic relation and as good as stated the pervading conception imposing form on the whole material out to its fringes of verbal detail, he can suggest no structural unity, but speaks instead of "looseness" and "matter more or less detached from the chief narrative" (pp. liii, lvii).

Klaeber has noted the outstanding instances of a circumambient structure, although the heading under which he groups them—Lack of Steady Advance—again shows that he does not allow the principle its fundamental importance. Most clearly in the fight with Grendel, but also to some extent in the slaying of Grendel's mother and the account of the dragon's hoard, we see the unfolding of an event into its separate aspects. Apparently, the sum of them all—synchronism and the momentary visual impression—is the one aspect not considered poetically significant. The course of the fight in the hall is several times reviewed,[9] each time in different terms and with varying emphasis. Grendel's movements and motives and his final sense of defeat are first described (745–57). The poet next reverts to Beowulf's grapple, considered as a fulfilment of his *æfempræc*. In 764–5 the climax, the tearing off of Grendel's arm, is obscurely stated in a metaphor.[10] The fight is then represented from the point of view of the Danes (765–90) who hear the din raging within their hall; the climax is here marked by the shriek of defeat, which is elaborated at some length (782–88). Lastly, the sensations of the Geats when they see their lord at grips with the monster provide an opportunity for contrasting Grendel's magic immunity from bite of iron with his impotence against the decrees of providence (801–15); these reflections are concluded with an explicit account of the severing of the claw, darkly alluded to before. The outcome for each of the three parties—Beowulf, Grendel, and the Danes—is then summed up, and the severed claw again mentioned, this time as the proof and symbol of Grendel's final defeat. A similar disregard for the synchronizing of the separate aspects of an action is seen in the defeat of Grendel's mother. Throughout the struggle the poet draws out the implications of each stage; he describes the virtues of the magic sword which Beowulf seizes in his desperation (1,557 ff.), occupies seven lines with the brandishing and victorious thrust, and next proceeds to display in one of his rare similes the flash of light which marks the defeat of the sorceress (1,570–2). The beheading of Grendel's corpse is also worthy of note. Much space is given to the retribution implied in this act, and the appearance of the huge headless body is touched upon: only in the final phrase is it stated *ond hine þa heafde becearf.*

Notes

1. 2,900–3,075.
2. 3,011–14:

> þær is maðma hord
> gold unrime grimme gecea(po)d
> ond nu set siðestan sylfes feore
> beagas (geboh)te.

3. 3015–24.

4. Contributory themes in the same manner are insinuated: Scyld's rich burial is contrasted with his destitute arrival, and the last state of Heorot with the first.

5. Cf.

hæbbe ic mærða fela
ongunnen on geogoþe

and the emphasis on *ana* (425, 437).

6. See also 50–2; 1,228–9; 1,408–10; 2,421–3; 2,602–4.

7. See also 194–8; 1,368–72; 1,477–20; 1,448–54; 2,356–9.

8. "Irregular, circuitous movements," p. lxv; "circuitous route," p. lxiii; "The thought of this passage, though proceeding by a circuitous route, is not obscure," note on 86–114: Klaeber's *Beowulf*, 3rd edition, 1936.

9. Cf. Klaeber, pp. lviii and note on 710 ff.

10. In support of this interpretation, *cf.* other instances of the concrete defined in abstract terms: *fela laf; wæteregesa*, "the terrible waters"; *fugles wynn*, Rid. 27[7], and the probable double entendre in *feorhlastas*, 846.

STANLEY B. GREENFIELD ON THE EPIC QUALITY

Although the digressions in the second part of *Beowulf* have been fruitful material for historically-oriented students of the poem, they have been somewhat unyielding to literary critics. The former have found ample sustenance in Hygelac's Frisian expedition, the poem's one historically verifiable fact; and with the aid of archaeological evidence and the testimony of Scandinavian saga they have drawn the battle lines between Swedes and Geats. The latter, concerned with structural unity and aesthetic decorum, have too frequently felt constrained to denigrate the second part of *Beowulf*. They find the fight with the dragon too much encumbered with "history", with retrospection and prognostication, as if the poet had not found his dragon combustible enough and needed more fuel for his poetic fire. These critics are more apt to perceive an aesthetic rationale in the digressions and episodes of Part I: in the tragic dramas of Finn and Ingeld, in the comparisons of Beowulf to

Sigemund and Heremod, in the poignant foreshadowings of Danish downfall. Even favorable criticism of Part II has largely relegated the historical material to a background or framework role, viewing it in approving but rather general terms. For example:

> . . . the whole elaborately investigated matter of the Geatish-Swedish wars, which seem to play so relatively large a part in the later *Beowulf*, is really significant from the point of view of the poem, as part of a lively and most moving framework or setting in which the rising tragedy of the hero can the more effectively be brought home—not only the tragedy of Beowulf, but the temporal tragedy of men in this world. Or one might say that these allusions and digressions, like so many others, help to give something of universal quality and meaning to the poem.[1]

That the *Beowulf*-poet has handled the events of Geatish history with insight and poetic power the recent researches of Adrien Bonjour and Arthur G. Brodeur[2] clearly demonstrate, and the observations which follow are designed, for the most part, to supplement their perceptions. First let us consider in certain historical passages the poet's selection of events from the totality of "history" in the poem, the themes he seems to emphasize in the different selections, and some aspects of the diction in these accounts.

Three passages in Part II of *Beowulf* conjoin Hygelac's Frisian raid and the Swedish-Geatish wars: lines 2349b–2399a, 2425–2515, and 2910b–3000. (There is a fourth reference to the wars which stands by itself, accounting for the provenience of Wiglaf's sword. This passage structurally balances an earlier reference to Hygelac's death in Part I of the poem.) The circumstances of the Frisian Fall come easily to mind: Hygelac's at-first-successful foray and ultimate defeat by the Hetware, Beowulf's revenge on Hygelac's slayer, and the champion's escape over the sea with thirty suits of armor. The Northern wars offer more trouble to the memory. As Miss Whitelock remarks, "The poet's account of these matters is scattered, and out of chronological order, so that modern readers find it difficult to gather the sequence of events without the aid of pencil and paper".[3] It may not be amiss, therefore, to set down briefly the dramatis personae and chronology of events in these wars, that we may see the historic totality plain.

On the Geatish side, the principal actors are King Hrethel and his sons Herebeald, Haethcyn, and Hygelac; Hygelac's wife Hygd and son Heardred; and Beowulf, Hygelac's nephew. On the Swedish side are King Ongentheow and his sons Ohthere and Onela, and Ohthere's sons Eanmund and Eadgils. The wars begin after Hrethel's death from sorrow over the unavenged and unavengeable death of his eldest son. With Haethcyn on the Geatish throne, an attack is made, but as to who dared first presume, critics still debate (see note 13). The upshot is the battle at Ravenswood in Sweden, where Ongentheow kills Haethcyn and threatens to exterminate his followers. But when Hygelac comes to the aid of his brother, Ongentheow prudently retreats into his fortress. But retreat is insufficient, and there he is killed by the Geat brothers Wulf and Eofor, whom Hygelac rewards handsomely. The first phase of the feud is ended, with the Geats victorious.

Ohthere rules in Sweden when Hygelac, now King of the Geats, makes his fatal raid on the Franks. He rules, too, during the period of Beowulf's regency. But when Heardred reaches maturity and occupies his rightful place as king, Onela, much to the wintry discontent of Ohthere's son Eanmund, occupies the Swedish throne. Eanmund and his brother Eadgils, revolting against their uncle, are forced to flee; they take refuge with Heardred in Geatland. Onela pursues, and having killed Eanmund and his Geatish protector, he departs, leaving Beowulf to rule the Geats. In *uferan dōgrum* Beowulf supports Eadgils against Onela, avenging Heardred's death when Onela falls. Finally, with Beowulf's own death in the fight with the dragon, it is predicted that the Swedes will again attack, and this time destroy the Geats as a nation.

So much for a chronological reconstruction. But how do we actually learn about the historic events? How may we construe their segmented presentation in the three passages under consideration? We may first note, with Brodeur,[4] that the three accounts are presented from different points of view: the poet's, Beowulf's, and Wiglaf's Messenger's. . . .

Passage III (lines 2910b–3000), the third point of view on the wars, is part of the speech of Wiglaf's Messenger. Unlike the first two passages, it does not move chronologically. First the Messenger alludes to the Fall of Hygelac; then he moves back in time to give the longest exposition of the first phase of the wars between Swedes and Geats, supplying the needed details in the Ongentheow-Haethcyn-Eofor battles. This order of events stresses the conflict in the North as the ultimate source of Geatish destruction. Thematically, the Messenger's speech has a double concern: presumption and rewards. Whereas the poet, in referring to the Fall of Hygelac, had focused on Beowulf's survival, and Beowulf had emphasized revenge, the Messenger views the outcome of the action as a result of Hygelac's arrogance[9] in making the raid; and in his account of the Swedish-Geatish feud, he finds the Geats presumptuous and the *causa belli*.[10] He dwells on Hygelac's inability to give treasure when he was killed in Frisia, contrasting with his largess in rewarding Eofor and Wulf for their dispatching of Ongentheow. The Messenger minimizes the concept of revenge until he begins his prophecy of doom: "Þæt ys sîo fæhðo ond se fêondscipe, / . . . ðe ic / wēn / hafo." His emphasis on arrogance vs. humbling and on treasures paid and unpaid suits the context of his speech very well: the death of Beowulf and the renewal of feud begun in arrogance and ending in loss of treasure to all—the maiden who will tread a foreign land deprived of gold, the reburial of the cursed and useless treasure, and the ultimate loss of *glēodrēam* to all the Geats.

The apparent contradictions between Passages II and III (and the earlier reference to Hygelac's Fall) may best be viewed, I think, in terms of their speakers and contexts. Since Beowulf, in Passage II, is intent on revenge as he prepares his attack on the old night-flyer, it is aesthetically suitable and psychologically proper that he single out his revenge on Daeghrefn in talking about Hygelac's Fall, that he blame the sons of Ongentheow for starting the Northern feud, and that he give credit obliquely to Hygelac *in propria persona* for avenging Haethcyn's death. It is understandable, too, that he should intimate that he prevented the famous necklace from passing into the hands of the Franks. He is a Germanic warrior uttering his *gylp*, however subdued and elegiac the tone of that boast may be. The Messenger, on the other hand, has another axe to grind. As a result of Beowulf's Fall, the Geats themselves will fall; and he is determined to locate the responsibility for the imminent disaster in the Geats: in their aggression against the Frisians, in large measure already paid for, and in their aggression against the Swedes, not yet fully paid for.[11] He bypasses the more recent phase of the wars, involving the sons of Ohthere and their uncle Onela—more a Swedish civil war, anyway, as Bonjour has pointed out,[12] in which the Geats got accidentally involved—in favor of the ruin and destruction the Geats in their arrogance carried to Ongentheow. Even if we accept Dobbie's reconciliation of the two different accounts of the start of hostilities, that "we are probably to understand that the first invasion was made by the Swedes . . . and that shortly thereafter Haethcyn initiated a war of retaliation and invaded Sweden",[13] the difference in emphasis in Beowulf's and the Messenger's speeches remains and is, I believe, aesthetically effective. Also, the Messenger, like the poet in Passage I and unlike Beowulf, achieves a fine balance of sympathy between the Geats, of whom he is one, and the Swedes, the traditional enemy, broadening our perspective once again as the epic draws toward its appointed end. If the passages are thus viewed, no real contradictions exist; we are presented rather with refractions of historical truth seen through the prisms of the speaker's perspectives and states of mind.

The *Beowulf*-poet's artistry is amply revealed in these three prismatic views of Geatish history. Where Olympian detachment sustains a theme of survival, heroic purpose lingers on revenge, and vatic admonition, in turn, sees beyond heroic presumption. The totality of such views and themes may well lead to the universal quality that Wrenn and others have noted. Perhaps it also contributes to the epic quality of the Old English poem.[14]

Coleridge has defined what seems to me to be a central attribute of epic: in epic, he says, Fate subordinates human will to its purposes; human will, in effect, subserves the larger ends of destiny.[15] Such a Fate-controlled universe we find in Homer, in Vergil, in Milton. Odysseus's will, for example, in a sense serves the purposes of Poseidon and Athena, and Hector stands before Troy's gate because Fate will have it so; Aeneas leaves his Dido to fulfill his destiny and Rome's; and Adam and Eve, though acting freely, are clearly attuned to God's providence. In *Beowulf*, epic effect is achieved differently. Wyrd and God may be repeatedly mentioned, but their force is less personal, less directive, than the Olympian and Heavenly decrees. The poem gives us no sense that Beowulf moves through his heroic deeds in accord with a higher will. Rather, Beowulf's is an historic destiny, as are all the doom-laden movements of the poem. The Scylding dynasty will fall—because historically it fell; the Geats will lose their national independence—because history records the loss. Wyrd will no longer grant Beowulf unalloyed victory when he fights the dragon—because the doom of the Geats is nigh. There is no "higher" destiny in *Beowulf*; and yet there is epic sweep. If there is a distinction and withal a similarity between other epics and *Beowulf*, it is in the kinds of destiny manifest; and it is precisely in the accretion of historical material—the many-viewed repetitions of the Swedish-Geatish wars in particular—that we are made epically aware. While the universal quality of other epics may reside in the assimilation of human motives and forces to suprahuman though basically anthropomorphic purposes, in *Beowulf*, it would appear, history subsumes the hero as an individual. This historic destiny, in a centrally significant way, universalizes and makes epic this Old English heroic poem.

Notes

1. C. L. Wrenn, ed., *Beowulf* (London, 1953, 1958), p. 73.
2. Adrien Bonjour, *The Digressions in Beowulf* (Oxford, 1950); Arthur G. Brodeur, *The Art of Beowulf* (Berkeley and Los Angeles, 1959), esp. Chap. III.
3. Dorothy Whitelock, *The Audience of Beowulf* (Oxford, 1951), p. 54.
4. Brodeur, *op. cit.*, pp. 83–85.

9. Most edited texts read *genægdon* "attacked" in line 2916b to avoid alliteration on the fourth stress of the line; but the MS. has *ge hnægdon* "humbled". Cf. the poet's account in Part I of the poem, in the earliest reference to Hygelac's raid, lines 1206–07a: "syddan hē for wlenco wēan āhsode, / fæhðe tō Frysum."

10. The passage is, I am aware, subject to differing interpretations. I follow Klaeber (*Beowulf*, 3rd ed.) here, p. xxxviii: "It is started by the Swedes, who attack their Southern neighbors. . . ."

11. The Messenger's emphasis on the Geats' past aggressiveness contrasts ironically with their unheroic behavior in the dragon fight. It is not just Beowulf's death that will precipitate the Geats' downfall, but report of their cowardly conduct, as Wiglaf had made clear to them. After all, Beowulf was old and would have died soon anyway; but there is bitter irony in the fact that the circumstances of his death gave the Geats the opportunity to show their cowardice, thus inviting their neighbor's attack. The Geats are responsible for their own destruction. Not enough emphasis is placed on this point, it seems to me, in discussions on the "tragedy" of Beowulf's death.

12. Bonjour, *op. cit.*, p. 42.

13. E. V. K. Dobbie, ed., *Beowulf and Judith*, ASPR IV (New York, 1953), p. xxxix.

14. For some indication of critical hesitancy to call *Beowulf* an epic, see note 6 of my article, "*Beowulf* and Epic Tragedy", CL, xiv (1962), 92.

15. Samuel T. Coleridge, *Shakespearean Criticism*, ed. Thomas M. Raysor (London, 1960), I, 125.

EDWARD B. IRVING, JR. ON NEGATIVE DEFINITIONS

Since a study of all the rhetorical patterns would be a book in itself, we must limit ourselves to examining a few important patterns. Most of this chapter will be concerned with negative constructions, since they have always been recognized as a striking feature of Germanic rhetoric. They surely play a major role in creating the impression of a persistent tone of irony and understatement that modern readers receive from this poetry, and they also have much to do with the usual representation of behavior in extreme terms. Particular attention will be given to that form of rhetorical heightening which is provided by the frequent combination of a negative clause or phrase with the adversative conjunction *ac* or with other words such as *hwæðre* or *swa þeah*, with the general meaning usually something like: "It is by no means A; on the contrary it is B."[2]

The poet may use negative terms to state or amplify his conception of what a true hero should be in two different ways. He may mention what a true hero is not or does not do (namely, bad things), or he may mention what a nonhero is not or does not do (namely, good things).

Let us begin by looking at some examples of the second kind of statement, in which characters or behavior more or less sharply defined as being the opposite of heroic are typically described. Two such examples occur in the passage in Hrothgar's sermon where the wicked king Heremod is described. Heremod is, to be sure, an antitype of the ideal king rather than of the ideal hero, but the passage illustrates the principle of the construction especially well.

> Ne wearð Heremod swa
> eaforum Ecgwelan, Arscyldingum;
> ne geweox he him to willan,   ac to wælfealle
> ond to deaðcwalum   Deniga leodum.[3] (1709b–12)

Heremod was not so [helpful] to the descendants of Ecgwela, to the honorable Scyldings; he did not grow up to be what they wished—far from it, he grew into the slaughter and violent death of the Danish people.

In such a passage we can sense the full rhetorical effect of this adversative form of statement. Here we have the energetic clash of powerful opposites: growth, potentiality for good, and the people's will on one hand; murder and destructiveness on the other. On one side of the *ac* fulcrum is stated (in negative terms) one ideal of true kingship: that the king grow into what his people wish him to be, or that he grow to become loved by his people. On the other side of the *ac* the two tautological compounds *wælfealle* and *deaðcwalum* put particularly heavy stress on the anarchic violence we actually find in this king. Heremod's brutality leads to alienation from humanity, as we see in the following lines:

breat bolgenmod   beodgeneatas,
eaxlgesteallan,   oþþæt he ana hwearf,
mære ðeoden,   mondreamum from. (1713–15)

In furious anger he cut down his table-companions and
comrades in arms, until at last he went off alone, that
famous prince, away from men's joys.

Keeping two opposites alive simultaneously in the hearer's
mind (in this instance, attributes of good and bad kings) may be
the most important function of this form of rhetoric.
What we find here, and in many similar passages, is a
form of statement in terms of extremes, where poetic energy
may originate in the violent oscillation of sense from one
extreme to another. Our second example, from the passage
immediately following the lines we have quoted, shows just
such an effect.

Deah þe hine mihtig god   mægenes wynnum,
eafeþum stepte,   ofer ealle men
forð gefremede,   hwæþere him on ferhþe greow
breosthord blodreow.   Nallas beagas geaf
Denum æfter dome;   dreamleas gebad
þæt he þæs gewinnes   weorc þrowade,
leodbealo longsum. (1716–22a)

Even though mighty God had favored him and exalted
him beyond all men in joys of might and strength—still
a bloodlust grew in his secret heart. He gave no rings to
any Danes to gain glory; no, he lived to be joyless and to
suffer pain for his violence, and longlasting affliction.

Here *hwæþere* serves as the rhetorical fulcrum. We are told that,
on the one hand, God, by giving Heremod the same gift of
heroic strength he has given Beowulf, has encouraged him and
raised him above other men. But Heremod suddenly turns to
evil, and to a particular form of evil (stinginess, not giving rings)
that is peculiarly ironic in view of God's generosity toward him.

The very willfulness of his behavior is signaled by the abrupt adversative transitions *hwæþere* and *nallas*. The expression "not giving rings" is in fact here a notable understatement, since Heremod apparently murders his subjects. We see the same expression later in Hrothgar's sermon, in the exemplum of the man corrupted by pride and the devil's arrows, a man much resembling Heremod:

> Þinceð him to lytel þæt he lange heold,
> gytsað gromhydig, nallas on gylp seleð
> fædde beagas, ond he þa forðgesceaft
> forgyteð ond forgymeð, þæs þe him ær god sealde,
> wuldres waldend, weorðmynda dæl. (1748–52)

What he has held for so long now seems to him too little; he covets fiercely—never any longer does he proudly bestow ornamented rings; and he then ignores and scorns the created world, the great share of honors which God, Ruler of glory, had given him.

Even if we leave murder out of the picture, avarice itself is always something more serious than mere stinginess in Germanic heroic poetry; it represents the immoral violation of a personal relationship that happens to be symbolized by the exchange of material wealth. In this light we may with some justice regard avarice as a form of extreme behavior.

Unferth, the Dane who insultingly challenges Beowulf when he arrives at the great Danish hall of Heorot, is in some respects another antitype of the hero. One negative phrase of the type we are examining is applied to him:

> Gehwylc hiora his ferhþe treowde,
> þæt he hæfde mod micel, þeah þe he his magum nære
> arfæst æt ecga gelacum. (1166b–68a)

Each of them trusted his spirit, that he had a great heart, even though he had not been honorable to his kinsmen in the play of sword-edges.

The past history of Unferth and his position at Hrothgar's court are by no means clear and may never be, but this remark by the poet, couched as it is in the habitual ironic mode of understatement, can hardly mean anything other than that Unferth has murdered his kinsmen.[4]

Again, the cowardly retainers who retreat from the dragon's attack and hide in the forest are certainly pictured as nonheroes:

> Næs ða lang to ðon
> þæt ða hildlatan   holt ofgefan,
> tydre treowlogan   tyne ætsomne.
> Ða ne dorston ær   dareðum lacan
> on hyra mandryhtnes   miclan þearfe,
> ac hy scamiende   scyldas bæran,
> guðgewædu,   þær se gomela læg,
> wlitan on Wilaf. (2845b–52a)

It was not long before those slow in battle came out of the forest, ten cowardly faith-breakers together; they had not dared to make play with their spears in their lord's moment of great need; on the contrary, in shame they bore shields and armor to where the old man lay, and they looked at Wiglaf.

Now that the dragon is dead and the danger over, they come forward quickly, although when they were needed they did not come at all.[5] But the negative clause here (2848–49) serves to define very plainly their primary obligation as retainers: to come to their lord's help when he has need of them. The clause with *ac* that follows presents a minor problem in interpretation, however. Precisely what is being opposed to what? If the emphasis in the preceding clause is on *scamiende*, is the chief contrast then between the retainers' previous shamelessness in flight and their present feelings of mortification? More interesting is the possibility of an ironic contrast between the help they did not bring when it was so urgently needed and the useless shields and corselets they now officiously carry to the place where Beowulf lies dead.

Another passage in which the retainers' duty is stated flatly and unequivocally by means of a negative phrase is the following:

Nealles him on heape   handgesteallan,
æðelinga bearn,   ymbe gestodon
hildecystum,   ac hy on holt bugon,
ealdre burgan. (2596–99a)

In no way did those war-comrades, those sons of noblemen, take their stand around him in formation as fighting-men should; no, they fell back into the forest and took care of their own lives.

This is again rhetorical statement in terms of the polarizing of possible behavior into two extreme kinds. The alliteration here of *hildecystum* and *holt* draws our attention to the alternatives: to stand in military formation or to go hide in a forest. As so often in Old English poetry, and in Germanic literature generally, this kind of statement vividly dramatizes a character's free choice of action, at the same time that a phrase like *aeðelinga bearn* reminds us of his hereditary aristocratic obligations. Heroic life is consistently presented as a series of such radical choices.

Another possible violation of heroic decorum, though in this instance certainly a venial one, may be the storm of emotion that overwhelms King Hrothgar when he says farewell to Beowulf, as the hero takes leave of Denmark and returns home.

Wæs him se man to þon leof
þæt he þone breostwylm forberan ne mehte,
ac him on hreþre hygebendum fæst
æfter deorum men dyrne langað
beorn wið blode. (1876b–80a)

That man was so dear to him that he could not hold back the surge in his breast; on the contrary, a secret longing in his bosom for the dear man strained against rational restraints, burned in his blood.

Beowulf's feelings on this occasion are not described. Assuming that he too feels some measure of grief, one may perhaps see a contrast between his stoical behavior and Hrothgar's yielding to the expression of emotion (a moment before we were told of Hrothgar's tears). But the more important contrast here is between youth and age (often referred to in this part of the poem[6]) rather than between heroic self-restraint and emotionalism. Hrothgar's long experience in disappointment has taught him that they will probably never see each other again; Beowulf is still too young to see the world this way. The rhetorical structure of this sentence differs somewhat from the structure of the previous examples, in that here we have a parallel rather than the usual contrast, for the ideas of the dearness of the man, the fight for self-control, and the hot wave of emotion are really to be found here on both sides of the *ac* fulcrum. Possibly the *ac* construction in this instance may serve simply to emphasize in a general way the strength of Hrothgar's feelings, since such a construction ordinarily suggests some form of emotional tension.

Let us turn now to some examples of the more common way of defining the heroic ideal by negations, this time by negating or denying the nonheroic. It goes without saying that courage is the most important heroic attribute; consequently there are a number of negative expressions that allude to the hero's courage in terms of his "not fearing" or not showing other signs of cowardice.[7] Not only phrases but compounds like *unforht* or (in *The Battle of Maldon*) *unearg* (uncowardly) fall into the same category.

In *Maldon*, as I have suggested elsewhere, constant reminders of the possibility of flight from battle do much to increase the dramatic tension of the poem.[8] There, of course, such verbal reminders operate in the context of a narrative that in fact describes mass flights. While the flight of the cowardly retainers does of course take place in *Beowulf*, it does not have as much relative importance in the poem; it is merely one dark background stroke in the tremendous heightening and brightening of the figure of Beowulf. Even though they are used less intensively than in *Maldon*, such formulas probably serve to keep alive at the edge of the audience's consciousness the thought that it is after all normal behavior to be frightened under such conditions.

From an assortment of negative phrases describing other nonheroic attributes, we might construct an interesting model of the Anglo-Saxon nonhero: a man who kills his companions over drinks and secretly weaves an ensnaring net of malice for others; who has a ferocious temper and the bad manners to find fault with gift swords.[9] Behavior like this may well have been common in England in the seventh or eighth century, perhaps even common enough to be called a realistic norm. But, since such speculation takes us beyond the bounds of our poem, it would be more profitable to examine these expressions in context. Three of them happen to occur in the same scene.

The final lines (2101–62) of Beowulf's report to Hygelac after he has returned to Geatland project an image of Hrothgar as ideal king, stressing as they do the grief Hrothgar had to suffer under the oppression of Grendel, the warmth of his affection for Beowulf, and, above all, his great generosity. The speech comes to its climax when Beowulf orders Hrothgar's splendid gifts to be brought into the hall and presents them formally to his uncle Hygelac. Hrothgar's magnanimity is used here (as nearly everything in the poem is used sooner or later) to reveal to us Beowulf's own virtues: in this instance, his love, generosity, and loyalty.

The occurrence of three of our negative expressions in this triumphant scene is of interest partly because it reveals what comes into the poet's mind as he contemplates uncle and nephew. A central theme all through this passage is fidelity, symbolized as usual by the exchange of gifts, and, again as usual, we are urged to think both of the affection that inspires the gifts and the obligations they entail. It is entirely characteristic of Old English poetic style that fidelity must be defined or set off or deepened in meaning by strong hints of its opposite.

In his presentation speech to Hygelac, Beowulf mentions that the arms Hrothgar has given him once belonged to Heorogar, Hrothgar's older brother, and that Hrothgar had not wished to give them to Heorogar's son Heoroweard. We are not told what Hrothgar's reason for this last decision may have been, but later versions of the story in Saxo Grammaticus and in the saga of Rolf Kraki make it seem at least possible that Heoroweard, like his cousin Hrothulf, may also have been eying his uncle's throne.[10] In any event the reference to the Scylding royal family must at least have reminded the poet of some plotting nephew, whether Heoroweard or Hrothulf, for otherwise the ensuing description of Beowulf as a nephew loyal to Hygelac would have had little point.

> Swa sceal mæg don,
> nealles inwitnet   oðrum bregdon
> dyrnum cræfte,   deað ren[ian]
> hondgesteallan.   Hygelace wæs,
> niða heardum,   nefa swyðe hold,
> ond gehwæðer oðrum   hroþra gemyndig. (2166b–71)

This is how a kinsman should behave—and not be secretly weaving a treacherous net for others or laying a deathtrap for a comrade. His nephew [Beowulf] was indeed very loyal to war-toughened Hygelac, and each of them was attentive to the happiness of the other.

This passage is a good example of the rhetorical effect we have been discussing. The semantic rhythm here is positive (*swa sceal mæg don*)—negative (the *nealles* clause)—positive (Beowulf's own loyalty). From a different point of view one could see it as constructed in another way: the first two parts are statements of ethical alternatives, while the third is a specific instance of choice. Beowulf has chosen one of the two possible modes of behavior.

What is done in miniature in this brief passage is done on a larger scale in the scene as a whole. Into this scene of absolute and dedicated fidelity in Hygelac's hall the poet introduces a flood of dark reminders of treachery in Heorot, chiefly through references to Hrothgar (2155), to Hrothgar's queen Wealhtheow and the marvelous necklace she gave Beowulf at the great banquet, and to an unnamed hypothetical nonhero who bears some resemblance both to Unferth and to the evil Danish king Heremod, as we can see in the following passage:

Swa bealdode   bearn Ecgðeowes,
guma guðum cuð,   godum dædum,
dreah æfter dome, nealles druncne slog
heorðgeneatas;   næs him hreoh sefa,
ac he mancynnes   mæste cræfte
ginfæstan gife,   þe him god sealde,
heold hildedeor. (2177–83a)

Thus Ecgtheow's son [Beowulf], a man known in battles, showed his bravery in heroic deeds, lived to gain glory; never was he the one to strike comrades over drinks by the hearth; his temper was never savage. No, with the greatest strength of mankind this valorous man kept safe the abundant gifts which God had given him.

Strength and courage are essential to the hero but they are not enough. Heremod and Unferth, both fatally undisciplined, showed their aggressiveness in the violent disruption of social order; Beowulf, while assuredly a veteran warrior, a *guma guðum cuð*, saved his fighting for the battlefield. The negative image of the nonhero is needed here for clearer definition of the moral requirements of true heroism, as they are embodied in Beowulf.

Elsewhere and in somewhat different ways, negative phrases are used to differentiate Beowulf from other men. The Danish coastguard's awed reactions to his first sight of Beowulf, for example, are largely conveyed in a rapid series of expressions that define the nature of the hero by excluding the expected, the normal, the usual, by saying what he is not:

No her cuðlicor   cuman ongunnon
lindhæbbende;   ne ge leafnesword
guðfremmendra   gearwe ne wisson,
maga gemedu.   Næfre ic maran geseah
eorla ofer eorþan ðonne is eower sum,

secg on searwum;   nis þæt seldguma,
wæpnum geweorðad,   næfne him his wlite leoge,
ænlic ansyn. (244–51a)

Never have shield-bearers arrived here in a more open
way, yet you were not sure of the permission of our
fighting-men or the consent of our kinsmen. I never saw
a bigger man on earth than one of you, that fighter in
armor. He is certainly no hall-lounger, unless his looks
belie him, his noble face.

How can the puzzled coastguard establish the identity
of these strange visitors? He can do it only by excluding
them from successive categories. Their behavior is entirely
different from that of previous visitors to Denmark, who
apparently have come either as deferential guests or as furtive
spies. But these men come openly and confidently; they walk
as if they already had the password. Indeed all the password
they need walks among them in the person of Beowulf.
And so at the end of this passage the coastguard singles out
Beowulf from the rest of the band: he is bigger, braver, of a
more resolute and heroic appearance. Yet it is interesting to
see how such a luminous and compelling image is constructed
out of negative expressions.

Later Wulfgar, who keeps the door of Hrothgar's hall,
further distinguishes Beowulf and his men from other visitors.
After a moment's inspection, he concludes that these men
are not only brave men but that they are responsible and
honorable volunteers rather than *wreccan*, that type so common
in Germanic literature, roving professional adventurers or
refugees from foreign vendettas.

Wen ic þæt ge for wlenco,   nalles for wræcsiðum,
ac for higeþrymmum   Hroðgar sohton. (338–39)

I believe that you have come to see Hrothgar out of sheer
pride and greatness of spirit, certainly not as adventurers
in exile.

53

Another negative construction (if we may take *forhicge* as expressing an essentially negative idea) sets Beowulf apart from ordinary warriors in respect to his method of fighting:

Ic þæt þonne forhicge . . .
þæt ic sweord bere   oþðe sidne scyld,
geolorand to guþe,   ac ic mid grape sceal
fon wið feonde   ond ymb feorh sacan,
lað wið laþum. (435–40a)

I have no intention on that occasion . . . of carrying any sword or wide yellow-bordered shield to battle; on the contrary, I will be obliged to grapple with the fiend with my hands and fight for life, one enemy against another.

Other warriors in heroic poetry make much of the process of assembling their weapons for battle, but Beowulf is different. The difference is most clearly dramatized in the half-ironic "disarming of the hero" scene just before the fight with Grendel, in the course of which Beowulf methodically divests himself of all the traditional accouterments of the epic fighter in order to meet the monster with his bare hands.

Finally, as king, Beowulf differs from others in his response to Queen Hygd's offer to him of the throne of the Geats:

No ðy ær feasceafte   findan meahton
æt ðam æðelinge   ænige ðinga,
þæt he Heardrede   hlaford wære
oððe þone cynedom   ciosan wolde;
hwæðre he hine on folce   freondlarum heold,
estum mid are,   oððæt he yldra wearð,
Wedergeatum weold.[11] (2373–79a)

None the sooner could the destitute Geats prevail on the prince in any way to become Heardred's lord or willingly to accept the kingdom; no, he [Beowulf] went on to maintain Heardred in his proper place in the nation by his friendly advice and respectful affection, until he [Heardred] grew up to rule over the Storm-Geats.

Placed in a situation of this kind, where the king is only a child, most men would yield readily to the reasonable pleas of their people to assume power. Many men would be only too glad to seize the royal authority. But Beowulf goes to the other extreme: far from plotting to seize power for himself, he devotes himself to keeping young Heardred in power by his friendly counsels. He will not accept a position that he thinks he does not deserve, even when it is freely (and probably legally) offered to him by a majority of the Geats and by their queen.

DEFINING THE MONSTROUS

Just as the hero can be effectively defined by the use of negatives, so negatives can serve to describe the hero's chief antagonist Grendel, especially in his relation to some familiar human norm. In fact it may well be that the essential reality of Grendel is best understood in terms like these, for in many ways Grendel could be called an instance of Negative Man. As a fighter and as a "visitor" to the Danish hall that he devastates, he is often treated ironically as a peculiar kind of human warrior. But he is set off from ordinary warriors in one respect, for example, because, as Beowulf points out, for all his courage and ferocity he does not even know how to fight with a sword:

Nat he þara goda   þæt he me ongean slea,
rand geheawe,   þeah ðe he rof sie
niþgeweorca;   ac wit on niht sculon
secge ofersittan. (681–84a)

He has no knowledge of how to fight properly, to swing sword against me and hew at my shield, even though he is brave in his savage attacks; no, tonight we must do without swords, the two of us.

Not only is Grendel cut off from the normal concerns of a Germanic warrior by his ignorance of the use of weapons, but he is further excluded from the ranks of noblemen because he has no father, or at least his father's name is not known by men.

> þone on geardagum   Grendel nemdon
> foldbuende.   No hie fæder cunnon,
> hwæþer him ænig wæs   ær acenned
> dyrnra gasta. (1354–57a)

People named him Grendel in the old days. They knew nothing of any father, whether any such mysterious spirit had ever been born for him.

Since, in all epic poetry, a patronymic is at least as necessary to a hero as a sword, Grendel's title to heroic identity is wholly obscured.

Unlike normal men, Grendel does not pay the Danish people the honor they surely deserve, but instead he obeys his own fierce impulses in disposing of them:

> Nymeð nydbade,   nænegum arað
> leode Deniga,   ac he lust wigeð,
> swefeð ond sendeþ,   secce ne weneþ
> to Gardenum.   Ac ic him Geafa sceal
> eafoð ond ellen   ungeara nu,
> guþe gebeodan. (598–603a)

He extorts toll, and honors no man of the Danish nation; quite the contrary, he does just as he pleases, butchers and sends to death (?), expecting no resistance from the Spear-Danes. But I am the one who will show him very soon now the strength and courage and fighting-power of Geatish men.

In this passage we see Grendel beyond the control of any of the Danes and equally beyond the control of any code of conduct that would be binding on noblemen.[12]

Grendel and his mother of course live somewhat beyond the pale, in a lake-bottom home which no human being has ever seen:

No þæs frod leofað
gumena bearna,   þæt þone grund wite. (1366b–67)

No one of the sons of men lives so old and wise that he knows the bottom [of that lake].

The range of human experience and wisdom cannot even reach the place where Grendel lives.

As was already suggested, several negative expressions of this kind are closely related to the poet's consistent and ironic presentation of Grendel as a mock thane, and serve to provide particularly compact and vivid statements of the irony. Grendel is first shown to us as a wretched exile from the human race, living in the darkness of social disgrace and spiritual isolation, perpetually bearing God's anger. Infuriated by the harmonious sounds of human joy in Heorot, he comes first as a "guest" to visit the hall; perhaps he is even viewed ironically as the good neighbor paying a social call on the new arrival (Heorot has just been completed and occupied). When the Danes abandon Heorot, Grendel "rules" there; it is in the context of a passage describing the wholesale evacuation of the hall by the terrified Danes that Grendel is called a "hall-thane" (142). But Grendel's authority in Heorot has limits.

Heorot eardode,
sincfage sel   sweartum nihtum;
no he þone gifstol   gretan moste,
maþðum for metode,   ne his myne wisse. (166b–69)

He lived in Heorot, that treasure-bright hall, in the black nights; but he was never permitted to draw near the gift-throne or the treasure because of the Lord, and did not know pleasure in it.[13]

Even though Grendel seems to be living in the hall, he cannot (perhaps has no wish to) approach the gift-throne—that is to say, make proper use like an ordinary retainer of the treasure for which Heorot is so famous. While the much-discussed phrase *for metode* might possibly mean in the presence of a secular lord (who is distributing treasure to his men), more likely it refers to God and hence suggests that a supernatural order in the world must finally set limits to the outrages of such creatures as Grendel.

In another well-known passage, the same kind of irony is used to bring out Grendel's distance from mankind. It is almost as if the Danes in the poem (or at least the audience listening to the poem) were being invited to try to bring Grendel into some meaningful and familiar pattern of reference, some relationship to the structure of human society. In this case the frame of reference is the Germanic wergild system of monetary compensation for wrongs done.

> Sibbe ne wolde
> wið manna hwone   mægenes Deniga,
> feorhbealo feorran,   fea þingian,
> ne þær nænig witena   wenan þorfte
> beorhtre bote   to banan folmum,
> [ac se] æglæca   ehtende wæs,
> deorc deaþscua,   duguþe ond geogoþe,
> seomade ond syrede,   sinnihte heold
> mistige moras;   men ne cunnon
> hwyder helrunan   hwyrftum scriþað. (154b–63)

He wished no peace-settlement with any man of the Danish force, and he refused to remove the deadly evil or to compound by making payment. No wise man had any cause to hope for the bright remedy from that butcher's hands! Far from it—that terrifying creature, the dark death-shadow, kept on plaguing them, young and old, tirelessly lying in wait and ambushing them, ruling the misty moors in endless night. Men do not know where such mysterious hellions go in their roamings.

The lines just preceding this passage have strongly emphasized the violence of Grendel's feud with Hrothgar (*heteniðas, fyrene, fæhðe, sæce*). But, as we see later in the poem in the story of Beowulf's own father Ecgtheow, human feuds can be resolved and peace can be restored, if the participants in feuds want peace. But *sibbe ne wolde*—Grendel does not want peace, nor indeed relationship of any sort with any human being, no matter how such relationship is (ironically) extended to him. Denied here emphatically is the (ironic) hope that he will abide by human laws and pay the fine for his murders, even though the idea is toyed with almost humorously for a few lines.

The verses that follow (here I assume that the *ac se* supplied by most recent editors in line 159 to replace letters lost from the manuscript is almost certain) move us abruptly, in the usual way of an *ac* construction, away from this temporary accommodation with mankind, this way of seeing Grendel as somehow human. A man as well as a monster could be called an *æglæca*, an inspirer of fear—Beowulf himself is called one in line 2592—but no man is a *deorc deaþscua*, a dark shadow of death. And then we move out quickly even further from the human center into perpetual night, the misty moors, all those areas beyond any ordering powers of the human imagination. As we cannot know his motives, so we cannot know Grendel's dwelling-places: *men ne cunnon*.

An ironic transaction of a somewhat similar kind is described by Beowulf in his report to Hrothgar on the fight with Grendel. In order to save his life, Grendel had left his arm behind when he fled. The act of leaving his arm seems to be represented as some kind of involuntary offering (and, if we take *feasceaft* literally, all he could pay) but this down payment nets him nothing.

> No þær ænige swa þeah
> feasceaft guma   frofre gebohte;
> no þy leng leofað   laðgeteona,
> synnum geswenced,   ac hyne sar hafað
> mid nydgripe   nearwe befongen,
> balwon bendum.   Ðær abidan sceal

maga mane fah   miclan domes,
hu him scir metod   scrifan wille. (972b–79)

But the destitute man did not purchase any comfort by
this action; the horrible plunderer, crippled by sin, lived
none the longer for it; on the contrary, pain had seized
him tight in an inescapable grip, in the bonds of death.
And in that place he must wait, that man branded with
crimes, to see how bright God will wish to judge him at
the Great Judgment.

Perhaps it is significant that the words *guma* and *maga*, common
words for man, are applied to Grendel in this passage, for what
is stressed here is Grendel's sinfulness (*synnum geswenced, mane
fah*) and his ultimate responsibility for his actions in the face
of the Last Judgment. However badly Grendel may seem to
fit the usual patterns of human society and behavior, he is not
an animal; in some higher scheme of order he is seen as human
and therefore responsible. Yet, just as the sacrifice of his arm
gains him no respite, his suffering and death gain him no pity. A
total failure as hero, he wins no glory or reputation in the eyes
of others; he does not even win their momentary sympathy:

No his lifgedal
sarlic þuhte   secg ænegum
þara þe tirleases   trode sceawode. (841b–43)

His parting from life did not seem pitiable in any way
to any of the men who looked at the trail of one devoid
of glory.

These curious ironic expressions, constantly bringing as they
do the possibility of Grendel's humanity into the periphery of
our consciousness even in the act of emphatically denying it,
have considerable importance in the meaning of the poem, as
we shall see when we look more closely at Grendel in Chapter
Three. For, despite all his inhuman and monstrous attributes, it
is ultimately Grendel's human ancestry that makes him the kind

of monster he is—the renegade who has deserted humanity to live in the wilds of exile, the frantic destroyer of the society he was once symbolically driven from in his ancestor Cain, the bearer always of the mark of murderer, and the bearer too of the mark of man.

Notes

2. Some remarks by Randolph Quirk in the introduction to his book, *The Concessive Relation in Old English Poetry* (New Haven, Yale University Press, 1954), probably suggested this general subject to me originally. I should make clear that the study here means to be suggestive rather than statistically exhaustive. Not all negatives in the poem are included, for example, although those negatives that are made more emphatic by the addition of some intensifier (e.g. *nealles, no, ne . . . wiht*) have all been examined. Enough examples will be cited to point to a pattern, but examples that are of no special rhetorical interest will sometimes be omitted.

3. The text quoted here and throughout (unless otherwise indicated) is basically that of E. V. K. Dobbie, *Beowulf and Judith*, Anglo-Saxon Poetic Records, 4 (New York, Columbia University Press, 1953). Dobbie's text has been somewhat simplified for the purposes of this book by the omission of his brackets and italics in those cases where he is indicating readings from the Thorkelin transcripts. I do use brackets and italics in the customary way to indicate emendations of the manuscript, however, and I occasionally modify Dobbie's punctuation.

4. The reader will find in Chapter Four [of Irving's book] a more extensive discussion of the larger context of this scene, the Great Banquet in Heorot.

5. The phrase *næs ða lang to ðon* or its equivalent seems at times to be a half-ironic way of describing a noticeably rapid sequence of events, as, for example, in *Beowulf* 2591 or *Guthlac* 903 ff.

6. For example: *ealdum infrodum* 1874; *oþþæt hine yldo benam / mægenes wynnum* 1886b–87a.

7. For example: *nis þæt seldguma* 249 (that is no hanger-about in the hall [but a fighter]); not being frightened but ... 2967b–69; not fleeing a step but ... 2524b–27a; not dreading battle 2345–49a; not flinching from violence 1537; not caring about life 1442, 1536.

8. Edward B. Irving, Jr., "The Heroic Style in *The Battle of Maldon*," *Studies in Philology*, 58 (1961), 457–67.

9. Respectively: *nealles druncne slog / heorðgeneatas* 2179b–80a; *nealles inwitnet oþrum bregdon / dyrnum cræfte* 2167–68a: *næs him hreoh sefa* 2180b; *nales wordum log / meces ecge* 1811b–12a.

10. See R. W. Chambers, *Beowulf: An Introduction* (3d ed. with a supplement by C. L. Wrenn, Cambridge, The University Press, 1959), pp. 29–30.

11. In line 2377 Dobbie reads *him*, most other editors *hine*, for MS *hî*.

12. In the latter part of this passage we may note another use of the *ac* construction that *Beowulf* happens not to illustrate very impressively. Here the *ac* is an expression of the heroic response, signaling the deliberate placing of Beowulf's will (or Geatish will, since the alliteration in line 601 surely reinforces the contrast between Geats and Danes) against this wildly [corrected] careening force of evil. Cf. also lines 1269–70. *Beowulf* has no other good examples, but this "heroic adversative" can be found in other poems; several of Juliana's speeches have this form (*Juliana* 105–16, 147–57, for example.)

13. See the note in the second supplement of Fr. Klaeber, *Beowulf and the Fight at Finnsburg* (3d ed. Boston, D.C. Heath, 1950), p. 465, and John C. Pope's remarks on this passage in his review of Arthur G. Brodeur's *The Art of Beowulf* (*Speculum*, 37 [1962], 415), where he paraphrases line 169b as "he feels no gratitude for gifts (or, as I prefer to think, no affection for treasure)."

T.A. SHIPPEY ON SYMBOLS IN THE WORLD OF THE POEM

A consistent fusion of tangible and intangible is built into the poem's scenery as into its words. Though the poet never says straight out that 'glory', 'worth', 'treasure', and 'weapons' are all aspects of the same thing, his phraseology does the job for him: Beowulf is *dome gewurþad* at line 1645, just as Hrothgar's saddle is *since gewurþad* at 1038 and the 'hall-man' (a tinge of scepticism here) *wæpnum gewurþad*, 'made to look worthy by weapons' at 331. Translation must inevitably be cultural as well as semantic. It is worth noting, though, that this complex of evaluations is not as alien as it might look. Over the last couple of centuries modern English has been busily developing the word 'prestige'. This meant originally 'illusion', but shifted during the nineteenth century in the direction of 'influence or reputation derived from previous character . . . or *esp.* from past successes' (so says the Oxford *English Dictionary* entry, published in 1909). Now, of course, it has become something possessed by men of power and (unlike honour) conferred very largely by the trappings of success—the 'prestigious' car, clothes, wristwatch, home-address. As such it has strong links with *dom* and *lof*. Admittedly, Mr Gladstone in 1878 called 'prestige' a 'base-born thing' and said specifically that it was not to be used in translating ancient epics. However, being 'high-minded' probably spoils more criticism than being 'base-born'. The word is a useful reminder of the way abstracts and objects can mix.

SWORDS, HALLS, AND SYMBOLS

We are liable to call such mixtures 'symbolism'. Indeed, according to the *OED* a symbol is 'something that stands for, represents, or denotes something else . . . *esp.* a material object representing or taken to represent something immaterial or abstract.' The coastguard's sword is a symbol, then, a material object which everyone takes to represent the abstraction *weorþ*. However, one can easily imagine a member of Beowulfian society insisting that this is not symbolism at all, just matter-of-fact. 'Look' (he might say) 'you wear a sword to show you're ready to fight, and people treat you politely because they can *see* you are. Distinguishing between being ready physically (swords), being ready emotionally (courage), and having social status (honour)—that's just splitting hairs! The three things go together, and if you lose any one of them you'll forfeit the other two very soon.' To return to modern terminology, there is a cause-and-effect relationship between the object and what it represents (like that between wealth and Rolls-Royces). The sword is an 'index' of honour—admittedly a stylized one—rather than a 'symbol' *tout pur*.[3]

This is not just a dispute over vocabulary. We need to keep in mind (as I have said already) that social signs in *Beowulf* function systematically, in systems which cannot be entirely, or even largely, the creation of the poet. The literary associations which 'symbolism' has acquired tend to blur this perception and hinder appreciation. Swords in *Beowulf*, for instance, evidently have a life of their own. The young retainer Wiglaf draws his as he prepares to help his king in the dragon's den; and the poet stops for twenty lines (2611–30) to remark on the weapon's significance. This one was not donated, but first won in battle and then inherited. Accordingly it is a reflection of the courage shown by Wiglaf's father and (given Anglo-Saxon notions of good breeding) a sign of hereditary worth. In the end it becomes totally identified with its owner's personality, so much so, as E. B. Irving has noted,[4] that it does not *weaken* and he does not *melt*—we would have expected these verbs the other way round.

But what happens if you inherit nothing? Since weapons are indexes of honour and status, deprivation of them becomes doubly unendurable. Beowulf himself imagines a scene (2032–69) in which a sword is worn by someone like Wiglaf who had it from his father; but this is seen by the man from whose father's corpse it was gloriously taken. '*Meaht ðu, min wine, mece gecnawan?*' asks a troublemaker [Can you, my friend, recognize that sword?]. He means, 'Are you a man or a mouse?', but neither Beowulf nor the poet bothers to explain this, since everyone knows the next act has to be murder. In exactly the same way the poet feels that the displaying of a sword to Hengest at the climax of the 'Finnsburh Episode' (lines 1143–5) will be self-explanatory. To us, as it happens, it is not; but we can see that the object prompts revenge with irresistible force and in total silence. In *Beowulf* objects can communicate whole chains of abstraction and reflection by their presence alone, and in a way felt by poet and audience to be too natural for words.

Some objects in fact reach 'mythic' status—most obviously, halls. What the poet thinks about these can be derived most immediately from his run of twenty to thirty compound words for describing them. Halls are for drinking in ('winehall', 'beerhall', 'meadhall'); they are filled with people ('guesthall', 'retainer-hall'); in them worth is recognized ('gold-hall', 'gifthall', 'ringhall'). They are also the typical though not the only setting for festivity and for poetry. It is this 'loud merriment in hall' [*dream . . . hludne in healle*] which Grendel hears and hates from the beginning, while Hrothgar's poet sings 'clear in Heorot' on every one of the three nights.

Beowulf spends there. What he produces is *healgamen* [the sport (you expect) of halls], and when the Geats look into their gloomy future at the end, the two things they fear to lose are their 'prestigious rings' [*hringweorðung*] and the 'melody of the harp' which, rather implausibly, used to 'wake the warriors' (from their beds on the hall floor, that is, see lines 1237– 40). Finally, whether it is from paint or firelight or candles, halls are associated with brightness. Heorot is *goldfah* [gold ornamented], and shines like a beacon: *lixte se leoma ofer landa fela* [the light blazed over many lands]. Inside it is decorated with glittering tapestries, *goldfag scinon web after wagum* [on the walls the webs shone golden], while at line 997 the poet calls it simply *þæt beorhte bold* [the bright building]. In the end the dragon comes to Beowulf's home 'to burn the bright halls' [*beorht hofu bærnan*], and there is a sudden striking image early on of Grendel prowling 'the treasure-ornamented hall on the black nights' [*sincfage sel sweartum nihtum*].

Already one can see how the 'mythic' interpretations come in. The hall equals happiness equals light. What do the monsters which invade halls equal? They are creatures of the night, 'shadow-walkers', 'lurkers in darkness', things which have to be under cover by dawn. It is no great stretch of the imagination to link their darkness with death. Meanwhile the poet's vocabulary, once more, shows an assumption that the happiness of the hall means life. In line 2469 old King Hrethel '*gumdream ofgeaf*' [gave up the joys of men], his grandson Beowulf (3020–21) 'laid aside laughter, *gamen ond gleodream*, merriment and the joys of song', the Last Survivor's kinsmen (2252) 'gave up this life, *gesawon seledream*, had seen the joy of the hall'. The compound words show how tightly men and harps and halls cluster together in the poet's mind, and presumably in his audience's. A similar familiarity informs the untranslated and possibly unconscious metaphor near the end, when the poet ruminates that it is a mystery where we all must go:

> þonne leng ne mæg
> mon mid his magum   meduseld buan. (3064–5)

[When a man can no longer, with his kinsmen, inhabit the meadhall.]

Meduseld is semantically indistinguishable from its familiar precursors *medoærn*, *medoheal*. By this time, however, what it means is 'Life-Gone-By'. The poet has no need to explain.

Halls are 'indexes' of happiness, then, because in them people are most likely to be free from poverty. They are 'symbols' too, because they are crowded with not entirely realistic conventional signs, like harps and gold and brightness. Their vulnerability implies a shared social myth about the limits of human capacity (stated most overtly by the councillor of King Edwin in Bede).[5] However, they remain at all times stubborn and solid facts, things which could be seen in reality as well as heard about in poetry. It is important that literal-minded Anglo-Saxons could always take halls literally, because what they would get from *Beowulf* was not the notion that Heorot was like life, but the more searching one that life was like Heorot. 'We too', they might conclude, 'live in a little circle of light. Every time we go to sleep expecting to wake up, we could be as wrong as Hrothgar's retainers. Æschere is us.' Involvement of this nature deepens many of the scenes in the poem. Modern readers no longer reach it naturally and wordlessly, but they are not completely immune to it either. Professor Tolkien's 'Golden Hall' in the second volume of *The Lord of the Rings* is still called 'Meduseld', and the name still has its power.

Notes

3. These distinctions, and others, are clearly drawn in Jonathan Culler's *Structuralist Poetics* (London 1975), pp. 16–20. Several of the points made in this essay form particular examples of the general procedure Culler recommends.

4. E. B. Irving Jr, *A Reading of Beowulf* (New Haven and London, 1968), p. 159.

5. Bede, A *History of the English Church and People* (Penguin Classics translated by L. Sherley-Price, revised edn Harmondsworth, 1968), Book 2, Chapter 13. See further Kathryn Hume, 'The Concept of the Hall in Old English Poetry', *Anglo-Saxon England* 3 (1974) pp. 63–74.

JAMES W. EARL ON THE GOLD HOARD

Since we have in the poem itself a digression on the history of the gold-hoard and its guardian dragon, we need not begin the project of determining their functions in the poem by searching outside the poem for analogues. In this digression, commonly called "The Lay of the Last Survivor," an old man, who has lived to see his whole nation perish and its culture fall into ruin, walks through his empty town; he laments the impermanence of the things of the world, and buries the treasures of his ancient civilization in the earth. These are the treasures guarded by the dragon which will ultimately kill Beowulf. There is a fundamental moral discovery attached to the old man's action, which is explicit in his speech:

"Earth, hold now the possessions of earls; now men cannot. Good men obtained them from you before; death in battle, deadly trouble, has taken each of the bold men of my race; they knew the joys of the hall, and now life has left them. O who might now wear the sword or polish the ornamented cup, the precious drinking-bowl? The warriors have all gone elsewhere. The plated gold of the king's helmet shall fall away; the treasure-keeper sleeps who would polish the war-masks; and the armor which in battle endured the bite of swords behind the breaking of shields, decays with the hero. The rings of the chain-mail will no longer travel abroad on the warrior. No longer the joy of the harp, the song of the instrument; no longer does the good hawk swing thrugh the hall; no longer does the town resound with the swift horses. Violent death has sent the race of heroes elsewhere." (ll. 2247–66)[1]

The history of the gold-hoard in this digression prefaces the main narrative of Beowulf's dragon-fight and is related to it in two ways. First of all, it attaches a moral significance to the treasure which the dragon guards. Everything we know about this hoard tells us that this is a treasure which should indeed be guarded; it is emblematic of the awful truth that treasure, and worldly achievement in general, cannot secure a culture against its inevitable decay. It is emblematic of the truth which the whole poem illustrates, that worldly success is only temporary, or perhaps even illusory. The dragon who guards this hoard does not seem necessarily to be a representative of evil. Rather, the beast serves the wisdom and the moral vision of the Last Survivor. And guarding barrows is the natural function of dragons—and a morally neutral function perhaps, as we can see in these lines from the Cotton gnomes ("Maxims II"):

> Masts are on ships,
> they hold up the sails; swords lie on the breast,
> noble irons; dragons are in barrows,
> old, wise, and treasure-proud; fish are in the water,
> they bring forth their own; kings are in the hall,
> they deal out rings. (ll. 24–29)[2]

Our dragon, then, seems to be morally significant, though not necessarily evil. In fact, in both *Beowulf* (l. 2277) and the gnomes (l. 27) the dragon is described as *frod* (old and wise). The most important question, of course, is why Beowulf has to combat the beast, and perish in the process. Let me just suggest for now that Beowulf's death is after all an illustration of the truth which the hoard represents, from the evidence of the Last Survivor's speech.

The second way in which the digression helps to clarify the significance of Beowulf's struggle with the dragon is that it is a clear prophecy of Beowulf's fall at the poem's conclusion. For not only are we told at great length that in spite of Beowulf's long and successful kingship, he and his race are doomed; but even more pointedly, we are told rather unexpectedly at the very moment of his death that he and his one faithful retainer Wiglaf are themselves, very literally, last survivors. Beowulf's last words recall those of the Last Survivor; he says to Wiglaf:

> "You are the last survivor [*endelaf*] of our race, the
> Waegmundings; fate has swept all of my kinsmen,
> valorous princes, to their destiny; I must follow them."
>   (ll. 2813–16)

Wiglaf, learning his lesson from Beowulf's fate, hardly needs further instruction; and like the Last Survivor of the digression, he too buries the gold, and "they let the earth hold the treasure of earls, the gold in the ground, where it lies even now, as useless to men as it ever was" (ll. 3166–68). And like the Last Survivor, Wiglaf does not bury the treasure for safekeeping—the English courts have even decided that question, in the celebrated case of Mrs. Pretty. The gold is not intended to be recovered; rather it is buried as an expression of a well-defined moral conviction—that moral conviction which the whole poem is meant to reinforce. Beowulf, his race, and his people fall victim at the end of the poem, not to sin, or avarice, or even evil (note that the Last Survivor describes his ancestors who won the gold as "good men [*gode*]"); they fall victim, rather, to the simple truth about life, shared by both Germanic and Christian tradition, that the things of this world *dreosaþ ond feallaþ*, they "fade and fall away," to quote both Hrothgar and the Wanderer. The transience of worldly things, of course, is not an unusual theme on Old English poetry, but its expression in narrative form in *Beowulf* is more elaborate and powerful than in any other of our poems.

In the history of the gold-hoard, then, we can see the controlling theme of the poem clearly expressed, and we can see how the poet explicates his symbols within the poem, with the aid of the so-called "digressive" episodes.

Notes

1. All translations from Old English are my own.

2. "*Draca sceal on hlaewe, / frod, fraetwum wlanc.*" *The Anglo-Saxon Minor Poems*, ed. Elliott Dobbie, Anglo-Saxon Poetic Records, vol. VI (New York: Columbia University Press, 1942), p. 56.

DAVID WILLIAMS ON CAIN'S PROGENY

If the thematic significance of the battles with monsters in the main narrative may be seen as that continual moral opposition required in the world against the persistent evil of fratricide, infidelity, and all antisocial crimes, then Beowulf is at once the anachronistic embodiment of Christian social values and a greatly endowed, if mortal, Germanic warrior in pursuit of the inevitably mundane, although praiseworthy, goals of pagan thane and lord. In his exceptional moral tenacity in upholding the values of kinship, comitatus, and peace throughout the poem he suggests the ideal Christian knight and king. He opposes the forces of social destruction embodied in the monsters, who are, of course, while embodiments of evil, individual enemies physically threatening their frightened victims and must be fought and destroyed in defence not only of moral principle but of life and limb, as well. Beowulf himself enters the contest with this pragmatic purpose, and as has been said, it is only gradually that he perceives the common origin of these harassments and their moral-historical significance.

This wider significance embedded in the main narrative is illuminated through the poet's use of the Cain legend. In making the monsters the progeny of the first fratricide, he is not adapting a self-conscious literary myth but employing an ethical and temporal scheme universally subscribed to in the middle ages, lending to his poem the metaphysical dimensions of the moral history of mankind. Thus in Grendel and the dragon the medieval audience of the poem would be able to recognize the survival of Cain's monstrous progeny and the symbol of his sin in those who formed the bestial clan dedicated to the destruction of social harmony and brotherhood and determined to eradicate the Abels of the earth. Herein one discovered the unbroken historical line in which evil had been passed down from the initial unnatural act of the first spiller of blood to the very present time, still haunted and persecuted by the monstrous offspring of Cain. The monsters thus represent the actual perpetuation of Cain's evil in the form of physical menace. Because of the traditions that surround them with an air of the marvellous, the same monsters evoke the fabulous. Somewhat irrationally, as with much legend, the monsters are both of angelic origin and human, their sire both Cain and Satan. Grendel and the dragon are both actual and fabulous, generalized rather than fictionalized, as representative of historical and moral fact.

The same theme of the evil spirit of Cain and the opposition to it is carried out on another level of the poem, for in the so-called digressions we see an extension of the idea to the modes of past and future history. These historical episodes, which constitute a considerable portion of the poem, extend the scriptural idea of moral history beyond the epoch of biblical time to the immediate past of the German nations and find in that history a corroboration of the scriptural and exegetical idea of the continuity of evil. They also provide a contemporary historic complement to the moral significance of Grendel and the dragon. In this manner the main action becomes a paradigm of the actions in the historical episodes and provides a universal explanation for them, relating Germanic history to that of Rome, Greece, Israel, and Eden.

The historical episodes are, then, not really digressions from the main theme but rather the means by which that theme achieves full moral and social significance and aesthetic completion. Having as the setting of his poem the historic present of the Danish and Geatish courts, the poet has carefully structured the episodes to reveal the universal significance of events in the respective national pasts and futures, moving out from the main theme periodically to past allusions and future prophecies in which signs already present in the main theme may find their mirror reflection in these episodes. The general facts of the Geatish and Danish past would have been known to an Anglo-Saxon audience since they constituted a history of interest to that audience. Thus the future as the poet reports it in *Beowulf* is recognizable to the audience as part of its own more recent past, and, setting itself in the present of the poem, the audience is able to accept as prophecy the allusions to the future, knowing, of course, that they have already been fulfilled. Having managed his poem and his audience in this way, the poet is able to reveal the ethical significance of history with the authority of history itself. Thus the episodes cover three Scandinavian sagas prior to Hrothgar's reign: the stories of Heremod, Sigemund, and Finnsburg. As R. W. Chambers has claimed, it is clear that in the literature and minds of Teutonic people a strong connection existed between Heremod and Sigemund,[1] and it is through this connection that the Sigemund episode seemed to form a part of the Danish past. Along with these are the prophecies concerning the Danish future: the treachery of Hrothulf and Unferth and the story of Freawaru.

Similar structuring may be noted in the handling of the tragedy of the Geatish nation. The past events of Haethcyn's fratricide, the Swedish wars, and the story of Eormanric extend the main theme to the past of this nation. Its future is evoked in the closing prophecy of the destruction of the Geats under Wiglaf. Thus the theme of the spirit of Cain described in these episodes, including historical examples from several Germanic nations at different moments in time, is presented not as a particular malady of an evil nation but as a fundamental part of the universal human social condition. Spanning past, present, and future of the time of the poem, the theme of the episodes seems to transcend time as well as place, and unlimited as it is to a particular nation, the evil of social discord is seen as part of the eternal human struggle.

On the level of the poem represented by the episodes, the children of Cain are not physical monsters but human beings who perpetuate Cain's sin, becoming his sons by adopting his spiritual disposition. Thus the transition between history and allegory is accomplished in such a way that characters are simultaneously engaged on both levels.

Note
1. Chambers, *Beowulf: An Introduction* 90–1.

LINDA GEORGIANNA ON BEOWULF'S SPEECH BEFORE THE DRAGON FIGHT

Just prior to his last fight, Beowulf delivers a long speech on the headlands above the dragon's cave (ll. 2425–37).[1] It is, with the exception of his report to Hygelac on returning from Heorot, Beowulf's longest and perhaps his most puzzling speech. Little has been written about the speech as a whole;

in fact, rather little attention has been paid to any of Beowulf's speeches, which is perhaps not surprising given Beowulf's stated preference for deeds over words. "It is better for a man to avenge his friend than to mourn much," Beowulf tells Hrothgar, and indeed in a heroic narrative we might ordinarily expect actions to take precedence over words. So it dismays those who would judge the poem primarily as a heroic narrative to find, as Klaeber did, that despite the hero's initial appearance as "an aggressive war hero of the Achilles or Sigfrit type," Beowulf is in fact "somewhat tame, sentimental, and fond of talking,"[2] and nowhere more so than in this speech.

When viewed primarily in terms of whether or not it "advances the action," Beowulf's speech before the dragon fight must seem inept.[3] Not only does the rambling monologue itself delay the fight, but the central story told in the speech concerns the sorrow and death of a hero and king for whom heroic action is delayed endlessly. Deferral or delay, evident throughout the poem in its style and structure, emerges here to become a subject of the narrative, suggesting that the poet's interests may not lie solely in fostering what Klaeber calls "true epic movement."[4] On the contrary, in the speech under discussion as well as in the second part of the poem generally, the poet seems intent on disengaging his audience from the forward movement of the heroic story in order to suggest the limits of heroic action and perhaps of heroic narratives as well.

In the Danish episodes, at least, action predominates. Beowulf's words in Heorot seem for the most part mere extensions of his deeds.[5] His boasts, while polite, are also fairly direct and squarely focused on the deeds of courage he is about to perform. References to history or to circumstances are subordinated to the promise of action. The poem's opening lines, "We have heard about the glory of the Spear-Danes in the old days . . . how those princes did brave deeds," herald in a major key the theme of old heroic deeds and the fame such actions have brought.[6]

But in what is usually regarded as the poem's second half or movement (ll. 2200–3182), the focus shifts. Edward Irving remarks that in *Beowulf* "history is made in Part I, while it is studied in Part II."[7] In the Heorot episodes deeds are done. Memories seem fresh, manageable, and close at hand, and although we sometimes see further than the characters— the poet's remarks on the devil worship of the Danes are a notorious example—for the most part such moments seem exceptional intrusions upon an otherwise unmediated view of Beowulf's glorious deeds. But in the poem's second half, deeds are talked about and meditated upon, described over and over from different angles of vision and at different paces.[8] The revisionary impulse seems at work here, creating a complicated context for the text of Beowulf's deeds by emphasizing causes, connections, and circumstances. In fact, so involved does the poem become in what could be called deep background that the central act of part two—Beowulf's fight with the dragon—is at times all but lost sight of.

In the first part of the poem one can hardly miss the fight with Grendel, which is prepared for with what has been described as fine cinematic skill.[9] In most cases everything but the poetic present is clearly labeled a digression, often in the form of a scop's song concerning some self-contained and chronologically remote episode.[10] But in part two, it is the present itself that seems the digression. Beowulf's fight with the dragon at times seems a thin, brief, somewhat dreamlike moment all but overwhelmed by the involved, repetitive accounts of past action and forecasts of the future: how the treasure came to be here, how the dragon came to be here, how Beowulf came to be here, and what will become of them all and the Geatish people with them. The heroic moment, the present, so significant at the poem's beginning, is in the second part almost bled of significance and reality as meaning shifts to the past and future.[11]

Nowhere are these distinctions between the two parts of the poem more apparent than in the poet's preparation for Beowulf's last fight. Nearly two hundred lines separate Beowulf's ordering his shield from his using it, lines dense with historical material spanning the history of the Geatish people. More than half of these lines make up Beowulf's speech, delivered as he sits on the headlands above the dragon's cave.

The hero's "gilp-cwide" of part one (ll. 407–56), delivered to Hrothgar as a tactful but confident piece of self-advertisement, is replaced here by a retrospective, highly digressive, meditative speech, less a preamble to action than an amble through various related and unrelated memories of childhood, both joyful and sorrowful, memories of the brave deeds of kinsmen and finally of his own glories as a hero. Out of this odd blend of elegiac stasis and heroic affirmation Beowulf shapes his resolve to fight the dragon. But the speech has a different effect on the audience, I would argue, distancing us from Beowulf's coming battle and from his heroic world, undermining the value and effectiveness of heroic action at precisely the moment when the hero is most relying on it.

The speech consists of a series of dissociated memories juxtaposed without comment: early childhood memories of Beowulf's happy youth in the hall of his grandfather, King Hrethel; the story of Herebeald's accidental death at the hands of his brother Haethcyn; the even more digressive simile comparing Hrethel's sorrow to that of the father of an executed felon; and finally a brief recalling of the Swedish-Geatish feud that follows upon Hrethel's death. Beowulf ends his reverie by reaffirming his loyalty to Hygelac, proved by his hand-to-hand combat with Daeghrefn, presumably Hygelac's slayer. The poet breaks the speech briefly here, then resumes with Beowulf's boast, which closely follows the phrasing of his earlier boasts, a promise to attempt to perform a "great deed" (*mærþu fremman*, l. 2514) and win fame and treasure.

The speech, which situates Beowulf for the first time in a personal as well as dynastic and national history, is treated by most critics as evidence of Beowulf's age and new depth of character. It certainly represents a side of the hero we have not seen before. For a character so often associated with the action of the moment, this speech represents a real turn in showing Beowulf reflecting in an almost leisurely way on Hrethel's sorrow and unheroic death. Beowulf's meditative mood is especially surprising in that he is virtually at the dragon's door. The hero has pondered his possible guilt, ordered his shield, assembled his men, and hastened to the cave; the time for reflection seems long since passed. John Pope explains the speech as the poet's way of representing the hero's old age realistically in terms of Beowulf's experience and frame of mind without having to portray him as subject to the "ordinary infirmities of age."[12] In Pope's careful reading the speech serves the double purpose of preparing at the same time for Beowulf's death and for his battle: the stories of Hrethel and the mourning father serve the first purpose, while the stories of more recent Geatish feuds and Beowulf's own triumph serve the second. Edward Irving further develops the relationship between these two purposes in terms of character, arguing that for Beowulf the case of King Hrethel serves as a negative example of his own current situation. Thus "the will to act is defined by its opposite, the world without action," a reading which might help to explain Klaeber's enigmatic note, "The king's morbid surrender to his grief is significant."[13] Although King Hrethel could find no remedy for his sorrow, Irving argues, Beowulf is still free to act and gain revenge from the dragon just as his kin did in the Swedish-Geatish feud. His meditation on King Hrethel and the nameless father causes him to hesitate but ultimately feeds his resolve to act, thus increasing his stature in our eyes. The poet, according to Irving, presents a new standard of heroism, involving sympathy and understanding in addition to "the capacity to act in total dedication." Eamon Carrigan, somewhat less sympathetic to the hero than Irving, at least sees Beowulf's turn from elegy to heroic affirmation as logical: Beowulf "now sees the acceptance of feuding as an escape from the elegiac hopelessness" of Hrethel's death. Rejecting despair, he quickly recalls those kin who could and did gain vengeance and fame, Haethcyn for the attack by the Swedes, Hygelac for the death of Haethcyn, and Beowulf himself for the death of Hygelac. Such memories propel him toward his final boast announcing his intention of performing a deed of fame.[14]

Such interpretations, which emphasize the psychological coherence of the speech and its function as a preamble to the poem's final action, are useful and are preferable to the critical tendency to treat apparent inconsistencies or shifts in point of view in this poem as evidence, in and of themselves, of interpolation, loss of lines in the manuscript, or a happy disregard for coherence.[15] Yet there is also a danger in underplaying inconsistencies and gaps in this poem, especially when it is done in the name of "realistic" character development. In reading the speech as an indication of Beowulf's maturity, readers have to work hard to smooth out inconsistencies, supply needed transitions and logic, and in general remold the speech into a more modern "dramatic monologue"[16] than perhaps it is. For Beowulf is not Prince Hamlet, nor was he meant to be.[17] His transitions connecting joyful childhood memories to the tragedy of Herebeald's death, the mourning of the nameless father, King Hrethel's death, and the Swedish-Geatish feud are by no means smooth, but rather abrupt, confusing, and disorienting. They tell us more about the poet's methods and habits of mind than Beowulf's growing sensitivity to sorrow. The emphasis on delay, introspection, and indirection describes the Beowulf poet more aptly than Beowulf the character; indeed certain parts of the speech, such as the reference to Hrethel's having "chosen God's light," are distinctly out of character, and thus all the more disconcerting to an audience.[18] A better explanation for the structure and subject of the speech lies not in Beowulf's character but rather in the poet's method, particularly in the poem's second half, of disorienting his audience by suddenly shifting the terms of his story. The effect, rather than encouraging a closer sympathy with Beowulf in his old age, is to force the audience to distance itself from the hero and the action of the narrative present. In short, the poet engages in what might nowadays be called a revolt against the narrativity of the poem's first half. He frustrates our desire for narrative progress and logic even as he frustrates his hero's need for clarity of vision and purpose in this speech, which is itself an interruption of the narrative and, in addition, has as its subject a hero's inability to act as a heroic narrative would require. This is not a new idea. What now might be called antinarrativity was described years ago in a famous section of Klaeber's commentary titled "Lack of Steady Advance." What is new is the modern or postmodern taste for subversive elements in narratives. For Klaeber, they were simply "trying."[19]

Notes

1. All references are to line numbers as given in the edition of Frederick Klaeber, *Beowulf and the Fight at Finnsburg*, 3rd ed. with 1st and 2nd suppls. (Boston, 1950), hereafter cited as Klaeber.

2. Ibid., p. 1.

3. Andreas Heusler's influential essay, "Der Dialog in der altgermanischen erzählenden Dichtung," *Zeitschrift für deutsches Altertum* 46 (1902), 189–284, rpt. in Heusler's *Kleine Schriften*, 2, ed. Stefan Sonderegger (1969), pp. 611–89, divides all of the speeches in *Beowulf*, and even parts of speeches, into two categories: "active" speeches, which advance the action, and "reflective" speeches, which retard action. Klaeber, pp. lv–lvi, follows Hensler and concludes that although the poet makes "felicitous use" of discourse in the poem's first part, where in general dialogue advances "true epic movement," the lack of "battle challenge and defiance in the poem's later speeches is an obvious, inherent defect in our poem." For a less narrow treatment of the poem's speeches, which also draws upon Hensler's work, see E. G. Stanley, "The Narrative Art of Beowulf," in *Medieval Narrative: A Symposium*, ed. Hans Bekker-Nielsen et al. (Odense, 1979), pp. 67–72.

4. P. lvi.

5. Just before Beowulf reaches for Grendel in the hall at Heorot, he recalls his boast and immediately acts on it: "Gemunde þa se goda, mæg Higelaces, / æfenspræce uplang astod / ond him fæste wiðfeng" (ll. 758–60). On the topos of words and deeds, see T. A. Shippey, *Beowulf*, Studies in English Literature 70 (London, 1978), pp. 12–14, and Stanley B. Greenfield, "Of Words and Deeds: The Coastguard's Maxim Once More," in *The Wisdom of Poetry: Essays in Early English Literature in Honor of Morton W. Bloomfield*, ed. Larry D. Benson and Siegfried Wenzel (Kalamazoo, 1982), pp. 45–51.

6. "Hwæt, we Gar-dena in geardagum, / . . . þrym gefrunon, / hu ða æþelingas ellen fremedon!" E.G. Stanley discusses the ways in which meter as well as language emphasizes deeds in these lines in "Beowulf," *Continuations and Beginnings: Studies in Old English Literature*, ed. E. G. Stanley (London, 1966), p. 112.

7. *A Reading of Beowulf* (New Haven, 1968), p. 201; see also pp. 195–206.

8. On the poet's interest in retelling, see Fred C. Robinson, *Beowulf and the Appositive Style* (Knoxville, 1985), pp. 25–27. Robinson argues persuasively that the poet's "appositive style" works throughout the poem, forcing the audience continually to

hold several points of view in mind simultaneously and to readjust its understanding of what is being described as it reflects on the differences between what appear as parallel statements. Similarly E. G. Stanley would seem to make no distinction between the two parts of the poem in his stimulating treatment of the Beowulf poet's penchant for indirection and delay; see "The Narrative Art of Beowulf," pp. 58–81. However, both Irving (*A Reading*) and Klaeber (pp. liii–lviii), in spite of their disagreements concerning the effects, would agree that part two of the poem emphasizes action far less than the Heorot episodes. See also the thoughtful treatment of the poet's narrative method in part two by Howell D. Chickering, *Beowulf: A Dual-Language Edition* (Garden City, N.Y., 1977), pp. 359–60, hereafter cited as Chickering.

9. See Brodeur, *The Art of Beowulf* (Berkeley, 1960), pp. 88–106; Alain Renoir, "Point of View and Design for Terror in *Beowulf*," *Neuphilologische Mitteilungen* 63 (1962), 154–67; Richard N. Ringlet, "*Him Seo Wen Geleah*: The Design for Irony in Grendel's Last Visit to Heorot," *Speculum* 41 (1966), 49–67; Stanley B. Greenfield, "Grendel's Approach to Heorot: Syntax and Poetry," in *Old English Poetry: Fifteen Essays*, ed. Robert P. Creed (Providence, 1967), pp. 275–84; and John Niles, *Beowulf: The Poem and Its Tradition* (Cambridge, Mass., 1983), p. 154.

10. On differences between the digressions of the poem's two parts, see Brodeur, *Art*, pp. 132–57, and the classic study of Adrien Bonjour, *The Digressions in "Beowulf"* (Oxford, 1950).

11. For an early treatment of the poet's manipulation of time in the poem, see Adrien Bonjour, "The Use of Anticipation in *Beowulf*," *Review of English Studies*, o.s. 16 (1940), 290–99. For some current critics, as for many of the poem's early-twentieth-century readers, *Beowulf* remains essentially an adventure story. Thus John Niles describes the design of the poem as follows: "If the reader does not become lost in the many byways of the narrative, the large-scale symmetry of its design will be evident: (A) introduction, (B) fight with Grendel, (C) celebrations, (D) fight with Grendel's mother, (C) celebrations, (B) fight with dragon, (A) close" (*Beowulf*, pp. 157–58). In the view of many readers, byways are a crucial part of the poet's design, not a deviation from it.

12. "Beowulf's Old Age," in James L. Rosier, ed., *Philological Essays: Studies in Old and Middle English Language and Literature in Honor of Herbert Dean Meritt* (The Hague, 1970), p. 5&. For a similar view, see Bonjour, *The Digressions in "Beowulf,"* pp. 33–34.

13. *A Reading of Beowulf*, pp. 223–29, here p. 227; see Klaeber's note to l. 2435.

14. "Structure and Thematic Development in *Beowulf*," *Proceedings of the Royal Irish Academy* 66 (1967), 34–37, here p. 36.

15. Signs of this tendency are evident in the notes to any edition of the poem which attempts to report the history of textual criticism, such as that of E. V. K. Dobbie, *Beowulf and Judith*, Anglo-Saxon Poetic Records 4 (New York, 1953), hereafter cited as Dobbie. For a historical study of the Germanic preconceptions which may have led earlier critics to reconstruct the poem freely, see E. G. Stanley, *The Search for Anglo-Saxon Paganism* (Cambridge, Eng., 1975). Those who would emphasize the great differences between Anglo-Saxon notions of a good story and our own include Kenneth Sisam, *The Structure of Beowulf* (Oxford, 1965), especially pp. 1–16, and, more recently, John Niles, *Beowulf*, pp. 163–76 et passim.

16. Chickering, *Beowulf*, p. 368.

17. See Kemp Malone, *The Literary History of Hamlet, 1: The Early Tradition* (Heidelberg, 1923), pp. 156 ff., and Adrien Bonjour, "Beowulf and the Tragic Muse," in *Studies in Old English Literature in Honor of Arthur G. Brodeur*, ed. Stanley B. Greenfield (Eugene, Ore., 1963), pp. 129–35.

18. See below, pp. 849–50. J. R. R. Tolkien, "*Beowulf*: The Monsters and the Critics," *Proceedings of the British Academy* 22 (1936), 286, considers this phrase the poem's "chief defect" of the kind involving putting Christian references "inadvertently in the mouth of a character conceived as a heathen." For an opposing view, see John Norton, "Tolkien, Beowulf, and the Poet: A Problem in Point of View," *English Studies* 48 (1967), 527–31.

19. P. lvii. On the often-quoted phrase "lack of steady advance," see Stanley, "The Narrative Art of Beowulf." Examples of modernist interest in antinarrative elements can be conveniently found in most of the essays gathered in W. J. T. Mitchell, ed., *On Narrative* (Chicago, 1981). In particular see the essays of Hayden White, Frank Kermode, Paul Ricoeur, and Robert Scholes.

SUSANNE WEIL ON FREE WILL

Who is the "Shaper" in *Beowulf*? Is it *wyrd*, the fixed fate that shaped the pagan world of the Anglo-Saxons? Or is it the Christian God whose worship they adopted? As the story of Beowulf was told and retold through the centuries, it seems to have picked up the verbal vestiges of cultural change like a snowball rolling through time: so many pagan and Christian ideas exist side by side in the poem that critics have long argued whether it is essentially a pagan or a Christian work. Some insist that it is a pagan poem which Christian transcribers defaced with dogma; others contend that its pagan pronouncements are relics of a time its culture outgrew—the poetic equivalent of the human appendix. Neither view gives much credit to the poet's intentions and artistry. Is *Beowulf*, then, a literary fossil in which two opposing belief systems are frozen together, fascinating from the standpoint of cultural anthropology, but ultimately lacking a unified theme? Or does the poem contain a genuine synthesis of two world-views? I believe that the latter is true, and shall attempt to show how a striking pattern of "hand-words" helped the *Beowulf* poet to establish that synthesis.

To begin with the language itself: many words that express the concept of *wyrd* are derived from the Old English root meaning "to shape." *Gescipe*, "destiny," means literally "that which is shaped"; the verb *sceppen* means "to destine, to shape"; one of the most frequently used words for "God" is *Sceppend*, literally "Shaper." Since the motif of *wyrd* as the implacable arbiter of men's struggles resounds throughout the Anglo-Saxon canon like a perpetual minor chord, the synonymous nature of fate and shaping in Old English should not be surprising: the singers of the canon were always aware that the events of their lives had been "shaped" by a force (or forces) beyond their control. Given the primacy of tactile imagery throughout their poetry, their vision of destiny as a process of shaping is characteristic. It is as if their Shaper were a sculptor, carefully crafting the form of each man's fate, molding a rough edge here, a smooth curve there, until the work took on its final cast in the moment of death.

As monks moved into Britain and began to record Anglo-Saxon writings, the *Sceppend* was assumed to be the Christian God: but who was he before that? The Anglo-Saxon tongue existed before the Christianization of Britain, and yet the Germanic religion which had held sway there had no supreme Shaper. According to the Icelandic *Eddas* (the best record remaining of Germanic, and by extension of ancient Anglo-Saxon beliefs), the Aesir shaped the first man and woman from trees but had few of the other powers we normally attribute to gods; not even immortal, they were themselves hostages to *wyrd* in the form of Ragnarrok, the day when the forces of chaos would overwhelm them (Green, 17–28; 203–208). Life began in the Germanic universe with giants being mysteriously shaped out of vapor; the Aesir themselves came to being because a hungry cow licked an ice floe until her lickings inadvertently shaped their progenitor (16)—but who created the cow? Even the three Norns who spun and snipped the threads of fate for each man were shadowy figures, spinning, not quite shaping, apparently acting without a purpose of their own. As we push the parameters of the mythology, every possible explanation seems to lead to another mystery. The Anglo-Saxon universe seems curiously without cause, yet brimming with effects—all subsumed under the murky heading of *wyrd*, which remains a force, not a figure. Who, then, is the Shaper?

A look at the proliferation of pronouncements about the power of *wyrd* in *Beowulf* suggests an answer to this question. Beowulf, repeating the received wisdom of his age, says that *Gaeð a wyrd swa hio scel* (Fate always goes as it must!: 445b), yet also that *Wyrd* oft *nereð/unfægne eorl, ýonne his ellen deah* (Fate often saves an undoomed man if his courage is good: 572b–573). The narrator says that

> . . . þone ænne heht
> golde forgyldan, þone ðe Grendel ær
> mane acwealde, swa he hyra ma wolde,
> nefne him witig god wyrd forstode
> ond dæs mannes mod. Metod eallum weold
> gumena cynnes, swa he nu git deð.
> Forþan bið andgit æghwær selest,
> ferhðes foreþanc. Fela sceal gebidan
> leofes ond laþes se þe longe her
> onðyssum windagum worolde bruceð.
>   (1053b–1062)[1]

> [. . . he ordered that gold be given
> for that one whom Grendel had before
> cruelly killed, as he would have killed more

if wise God and the man's courage had not
forestalled that fate. God ruled all
the race of men, as he now yet does.
Yet is discernment everywhere best,
forethought of mind. He shall endure much
Of what is dear and dreadful who here
In these trouble-days long uses this world.]
  (italics mine)

In the first of these axioms, fate is unalterable; in the second,
it plays favorites; in the narrator's aside, it is subordinate
to *both* "wise God" *and* "the man's courage." Someone is
confused here, and I would suggest that it is neither Beowulf
nor the narrator: rather, it is the modern audience, tending
to miss the point of these pronouncements. Critics who see
the poem as primarily Christian (Margaret Goldsmith comes
to mind) view the narrator's pronouncement on the power
of God as evidence that Christian providence, not *wyrd*,
was the Shaper of the Anglo-Saxon world—ignoring other
pronouncements that the narrator makes elsewhere about
the supreme power of fate. If proving God to be the sole
power were the narrator's purpose, why would he immediately
append the caveat "yet is discernment everywhere best,
forethought of mind?" He seems to be telling his audience
not to count on the power of God or *wyrd*: the future will be
a mixture of satisfaction and suffering even though God (or
fate) "rule(s) all the race of men." What a man *can* depend on
is his "forethought of mind": this is the core of the individual's
power to endure. Pronouncements about the importance
of self-reliance outnumber pronouncements about anyone's
power: for example, when Beowulf discovers that his borrowed
sword cannot harm Grendel's mother, the poet tells us:

. . . strenge getruwode,
mundgripe mægenes. Swa sceal man don,
þonne he æt guðe gegan þenceð
longsumne lof; na ymb his lif cearað.
  (1533–1536)

[... he trusted in his strength,
in his strong hand-grip. So shall man do
when he thinks to win at war
long-lasting praise; he does not care about his life.]

Beowulf wastes no time wondering what fate has written about this battle: he thinks ahead to the reputation he wants to win and fights on. *Swa sceal man don* was not praise, but a cultural imperative which epitomized the Anglo-Saxon *modgeðanc* ("way of thinking"): what mattered was not who shaped a man's death, or when he died, but how he died.

This is where modern debates on the meaning of *wyrd* in Anglo-Saxon poetry go awry, for in considering whom the Anglo-Saxons believed shaped their fate, we need to understand fate as they would have defined it. The excerpt above strongly suggests that a man's reputation was as integral to his fate as the time and place of his death: that reputation *was* Anglo-Saxon immortality. Call it God's providence or the mysterious, ubiquitous *wyrd*: an arrow by any other name would kill you. Your choice, then, was whether you took that arrow in the back or head-on, and how you chose determined whether you would be sung as a hero, a villain—or not at all. Your reputation at death even affected your family's future, determined whether your sons would be powerful lords' retainers and whether your daughters would marry well. Most important, it was a matter of personal honor to be remembered as a man of courage. It would be a good fate, indeed the best, to die gloriously in the protection of your people as Beowulf does—an ignoble fate to live after deserting your lord, as Beowulf's cowardly retainers do at the end of the poem. Bravery in extremity, grace under pressure: these are choices, and these a man could shape. Because the Anglo-Saxons believed this, I would like to suggest that the power behind the words of shaping in Anglo-Saxon poetry was, in the sense that mattered most to them, the power of the individual.

The unusual preponderance of words meaning "hand" (hereafter "hand-words") in *Beowulf* supports my contention that the individual was the primary shaper of his fate in Anglo-Saxon poetry. *Folm, mund,* and *hond* are not commonly used in Old English (compared with words meaning "battle," "warrior," or "sword," etc.), and yet they appear sixty-five times in the 3,182 lines of *Beowulf* (a sizeable number of their 435 appearances in what remains of the canon[2]). Forty-seven of those appearances, a full two-thirds, occur in clusters during episodes in which Beowulf's life or reputation hangs in the balance, either in episodes of actual combat such as the above example (in which Beowulf trusts in his "strong handgrip") or in the scenes of his political testing at the hands of Hrothgar, Unferth, or Hygelac. I believe that these hand-words constitute an oral formula little remarked but crucial, for Beowulf, through the "strength of thirty" in his hands, transforms himself from the son of an outcast to a great hero and king in a culture where ancestry determined one's role in society. If Beowulf did not "shape his fate," no character in Anglo-Saxon legend ever did.

Notes

1. All passages from Beowulf are from Dobbie, E.V.K., *Beowulf and Judith*, vol. 4 of *The Anglo-Saxon Poetic Records*. New York: Columbia UP, 1953. Translations are by E. Talbot Donaldson and Stanley Greenfield.
2. See *A Concordance to the Anglo-Saxon Poetic Records*.

Works Cited

Beowulf: The Donaldson Translation, Backgrounds, and Sources of Criticism. Ed. Joseph F. Tuso. New York: W.W. Norton & Co., 1975.

Bessinger, Jr., Jess, ed. *A Concordance to the Anglo-Saxon Poetic Records.* Ithaca and London: Cornell UP, 1978.

Dobbie, E. V. K, ed. *Beowulf and Judith*, vol. 4 of *The Anglo-Saxon Poetic Records.* New York: Columbia UP, 1953.

Green, Roger Lancelyn. *Myths of the Norsemen, Retold from the Old Norse Poems and Tales.* Harmondsworth: Penguin Books Ltd., 1960.

Greenfield, Stanley B. "*Beowulf* and Epic Tragedy." *Festschrift on Old English Literature in Honor of A. G. Brodeur.* 1963.

———. *A Readable Beowulf.* Carbondale: Southern Illinois University Press, 1982.

Goldsmith, Margaret. *The Mode and Meaning of Beowulf.* London: Althone Press, 1970.

Stanley, E. G. *Continuations and Beginnings*. London: Nelson, 1966. 134–40.

Stanton, F. M. *Anglo-Saxon England*. London: Oxford UP, 1947.

Timmer, B. J. "*Wyrd* in Anglo-Saxon Prose and Poetry." *Essential Articles on Old English Poetry*. Hamden: Archon Books, 1968. 124–163.

PAUL DEAN ON HISTORY AND THE PASSAGE OF TIME

I

Whether or not the *Beowulf*-poet had read the *Aeneid*—the evidence is inconclusive—they have in common an enigmatic vision of the past. We can easily apply to *Beowulf* the terms used some years ago in a critical dispute over whether Virgil could be called a great poet of history as well as a great poet of time. Professor A.D. Nuttall thought he could not, because his approach was typological and 'the typological imagination is interested in sameness while the historical imagination is interested in difference', but Dr Stephen Medcalf thought he did have such an interest, praising his 'obsession with time, and his belief, or at least readiness to believe, that a new epoch with a radical shift in the nature of things, was happening in his own time'.[1] I am on Dr Medcalf's side about Virgil, and about *Beowulf* too, which I shall try to show is a great poem about history, and even about philosophy of history. This position is by no means widely accepted. Voices have been raised to deny historical consciousness, not only to the author of *Beowulf*, but to the Anglo-Saxons as a whole. For instance, Michael Hunter writes:

> All the strands of the past, Roman, Germanic, biblical or native, were knitted into single, comprehensive fabric [. . .] The past was visualized in terms of a heroic, idealized present [. . .] There was only one past for the Anglo-Saxons, one in which many traditions were vaguely confused . . .[2]

While Adelaide Hardy is still more dismissive:

The urge to create an identity through the illusion of continuity with the past is obviously different from 'historical sense', which depends on the desire to distinguish between fact and fiction, and the ability to place events in their proper chronological context. [. . .] It is to be doubted that before the coming of Christianity the Anglo-Saxons possessed an 'instinctive historical sense' which enabled them to preserve the details and chronology of events from the past; and it is more likely that they viewed the past through legends which gave a mysterious illusion of continuity.[3]

The last comment can be ignored as beside the point for a post-Christian poem such as *Beowulf*. Hardy quotes Tolkien's assertion that the poet had an 'instinctive historical sense', a point which he immediately sabotaged by adding that it had been used 'with a poetical and not an historical object'— whatever *that* means![4] He need not have been so cautious. One could begin to contest the views of Hunter and Hardy by pointing to King Alfred's translation of Boethius, so long despised but now at last beginning to be recognised as possessing its own intellectual integrity.[5] Boethius, like Virgil, was seen as a vital mediator between the pagan and Christian worlds, and, as will emerge, I believe his influence on *Beowulf* can be much more convincingly maintained than Virgil's. In one of the best comparisons of the *Consolation* and *Beowulf*, W.F. Bolton comments that

What the *Consolatio* addresses through dialectic and doctrine, however, *Beowulf* approaches through literary form: the artifact becomes an embodiment of the concept.[6]

Bolton here raises a crucial point—the relation of the poem's philosophy of history to its artistic form. The matter is of some theoretical interest, since a historical poet faces complex technical challenges. Within the time-scale of the subject-matter he must create a past, present and future, which must in turn be balanced against the past, present and future of himself and his audience, the relationship between the two time-scales frequently giving occasion for irony or pathos and lending itself to an objectifying or distancing of the poem's readers or hearers from its personages. A third dimension, beyond the poet's control, occurs after his lifetime when he, his contemporaries and his poem become history for a future generation. All this applies equally to the *Aeneid* and to *Beowulf*, both, in some sense, epics which incorporate the history (to be understood as including much that is not history to us) of their first audiences with the teleological aim of showing 'how we got here'. I do not agree with Professor Nuttall that teleology, and its concomitant, a figural imagination, preclude awareness of historical change. All we can reasonably say is that they *account for* historical change in a way which is no longer widely accepted. Yet that does not make them debased intellectual currency: Hegel and Marx were teleological in approach and continue to be taken more seriously than our poet!

Because he *is* first a poet, not an historian or a philosopher, critics have particular responsibilities when discussing the historical 'background' of the poem. and here, if I may say so without offence, it seems to me that *Beowulf* needs rescuing from its admirers. The historical references in the poem are part of its existence *as a poem*, not simply extraneous material of a different order of being. I do not say that the enormous amount of research into the historical allusions in *Beowulf* has been a waste of time, but I do believe it has been misdirected. The questions the researchers ask themselves are 'what are the historical events to which the poet refers here, how accurate is his knowledge of them, and where did this knowledge come from?' But clearly, if we want to respond to the poem as literature, the question must be 'what is the effect on the poem as a poem of presenting these details in this way at this point?'—and this question can only be answered by looking hard at the poem, not away in another direction. Further, the sheer perplexity induced in the hearers and readers by the elliptical nature of the allusions may well be deliberate. Scholars assure us that the original audience would have spotted at once what was being referred to, but we cannot know that that was the case, and it is at least equally likely that some of them were as baffled as we are. As events and identities accumulate, come and go, and merge into a dizzying kaleidoscope, the poet rams home the lesson that history is both an enigma and a burden. But if we are following a re-ordered summary we shall never grasp this. In short, the excavators of historical allusion in the poem have ceased to consider it as a poem. Professor Ruth Morse shows us a more excellent way in stressing 'what kind of representation of what understanding for what audience are essential questions to ask when evaluating medieval and renaissance history', and in reformulating the question in the poet's mind as 'on the assumption that something very like this might be thought to have happened, how are we to understand the events?'[7]

So too with the structure and the 'digressions': it is no use abstracting the historical allusions, re-arranging them in chronological order and giving a connected narrative, with the implication that the poem is structurally defective. The comment quoted above that 'historical sense' involves 'the ability to place events in their proper chronological context' begs the question, for there *is* a chronological context which seems 'proper' to the poet; it is simply not a linear one. He *chose* to proceed by indirections and we are told what we need to know when he thinks we need to know it and not before, in the way in which he thinks we need to know it and in no other way. Leyerle was right: 'there are no digressions in *Beowulf*'.[8]

It was again Tolkien who pointed to an illuminating approach to the poem's structure, although again his phrasing was unhappy. In a celebrated passage in his 1936 lecture he stated that *Beowulf*

is essentially a balance, an opposition of ends and beginnings. In its simplest terms it is a contrasted description of two moments in a great life, rising and setting; an elaboration of the ancient and intensely moving contrast between youth and age, first achievement and final death. It is divided in consequence into two opposed portions, different in matter, manner and length.[9]

Tolkien's 'simplest terms' were too simple. Kenneth Sisam rightly objected that 'it is not clear what beginnings in the first part and what ends in the latter part are opposed', and Bolton warns against making 'a leap from the demonstrated formal properties of the poem to the predicted thematic properties'.[10] Yet this binary principle of construction has been detected in other Old English poems such as *The Wanderer* and *The Seafarer*, as well as in the *Aeneid* and other classical literature.[11] There may be cause for saying that it is not only present, but functionally present, in *Beowulf*.

Tolkien's statement is open to objection not because he says something is there which is not there (everyone agrees that there is a major structural break at line 2200, and I shall use this as a dividing point between this essay and its continuation) but because he says it works in a way in which it does not. For his 'simplest terms' collapse into a single moment of apprehension or realisation what is in fact a gradual dawning of awareness in the reader's mind, a process which it requires the architectural development of the whole poem to enact. His connection of the binary structure with the half-line, later in his lecture, was a surer intuition; for *Beowulf* is a remarkable case of a poem whose microcosmic and macrocosmic structures reinforce one another. Its stylistic preference for parataxis over subordination matches its fondness for significant collocation rather than sequential narrative. The best word for the relationship between its vision of the past and its, structural technique is Donne's: 'interinanimation'.

So far I have been mainly concerned with critical opinion, but in the rest of the essay I wish to concentrate on what we can deduce from the text itself about the poet's view of the past. This old New Critical procedure may have value in this case, however, because, despite continuing debate, we actually have no idea when or where the poem was written,[12] and to attempt: to relate the events it incorporates to some proposed 'contemporary' context may be at best a circular argument, at worst a distracting irrelevance.

II

The poem opens with a demand for our attention *now* which is immediately followed by an appeal to our common *past* experience, specifically our memory of certain kinds of story— 'Hwæt we [. . .] gefrunon'—and *what* we have heard of is also remote from us in time—'Gar-Dena | in geardagum/þeod-cyninga | þrym' (1–2). Syntactically, as my fragmenting of the quotation shows, the past is wrapped round by communal memory.

The management of time in the 'Prologue', the first fifty lines or so, induces in us a sense of temporal dislocation characteristic of de poem as a whole. The story of Scyld is narrated in a rapid impressionistic way, with ambiguous or vague temporal indications such as 'aerest', 'oðþaet', 'æfter', 'lange hwile', 'lange ahte' (6, 9, 12, 16, 31).[13] The brisk sketch of the conquests which consolidated his leadership comes to a temporary point of stasis in the exclamation 'þæt wæs god cyning' (11) which gives 'an impression of finality in a summarizing statement'"[14] and is later used of Hrothgar and Beowulf himself (863, 2390). This is a good moment to dispose of another vexed question, that of 'formulaic phrases'. The fact that a phrase is used more than once does not empty it of meaning: on the contrary, each repetition is coloured by its predecessors and acquires an extra dimension of meaning. So, here, the phrase establishes, across great tracts of the poem, a parallelism of character which also makes us think about the implications of 'god' in each case. After its use at 11 a new indefinite movement gets under way with 'æfter' (12) as the valour of Scyld's son Beowulf is praised. All the editors solemnly remind us that this Beowulf is is not the eponymous hero, but that is exactly the point, and when the hero does finally say 'Beowulf is min nama' (343) the poet has engineered a momentary confusion which again points up the parallels.

From these long stretches of time we swoop on particular moment as Scyld dies 'to gescæp-hwile' (26), 'at the appointed hour' (appointed by whom?), introducing the first lengthy concentration on a specific event—a funeral, anticipating the end of the poem. Scyld's burial is telescoped together with his initial voyage, as a baby, in a moment which does provide some justification for Tolkien's comments quoted earlier:

Naelæs hi hine læssan   lacum teodan,
þeod-gestreonum,   þon þa dydon,
þe hine æt frumsceafte   forð onsendon
ænne ofer yðe   umbor-wesende (43–6)

The use of 'frumscæfte', also found in line 91 and in Caedmon's Hymn to mean the creation of the world, lends an aura of immense age to Scyld; his life is both unimaginably long and compressed into a single instant, a brief interval between two voyages into the unknown.

From 53 his success story seems due to be repeated—and consolidated, for this figure who came from nowhere and had no past, whose very name is a symbol of his function, is now the founder of a burgeoning dynasty. Time moves rapidly on: we hear of Hrothgar's birth in 61 and of his military leadership in 64:

þa wæs Hroðgare   here-sped gyfen,
wiges weorð-mynd,   þæt him his wine-magas
georne hyrdon,   oððþæt seo geogoð geweox
mago-driht micel.   Him on mod be-arn
þæt heal-reced   hatan wolde. . . (64–8)

'þa', 'þxt' and 'oððþaet' continue the temporal vagueness, but the caesura in 67 marks a decisive break. From the acts which confirm Hrothgar's leadership we move to an idea; out of the flux of time emerges the imposition of an individual will, a will not merely to build a hall but to create something historically new, unprecedented—

medo-ærn micel   men gewyrcean,
þonne yldo bearn   æfre gefrunon (69–70)

—which will involve many peoples beside Hrothgar's own (74–6). The hall, symbol of Hrothgar's success and of civilization, rises miraculously from nothing, in due time but in human eyes quickly (76f.). The speed gives an impression of Hrothgar's power; he has only to command and his bidding is done. But the poet no sooner presents the hall, 'towering high' (are we to think of Babel?) than he sounds an ominous note: Heorot

> heaðo-wylma bad,
> laðan liges;   ne wæs hit lenge þa gen,
> þaet se ecg-hete   aþum-swerian
> æfter wæl-niðe   wæcnan scolde. (83–5)

This device recurs (e.g. 1017–9); by assuring us that something had not yet occurred the poet makes us aware of its inevitability—a simultaneous postponement and prophecy of doom.

From human creation, destined to crumble in time, the perspective moves to Divine creation and the establishment of an eternal order. The stop sings of history impregnated with spirituality, recounting 'frumsceaft fira | feorran' (91), celebrating the harmony of the cosmos and the plenitude of the created world in which God 'lif eac gesceop/cynna gehwylcum, | þara ðe cwice hwyrfaþ' (97f.). The insistence on 'gehwylcum' immediately introduces a problem, for the scop's song is sandwiched in between the first references to Grendel, and the double nature of 'creation' soon becomes clear: from the archetypal fratricide of Cain all the internecine strife in the poem descends, and Grendel, Cain's descendant, is the product and embodiment of a grim anti-creation, a horrible parody of human society, with its own kinship bonds and complex etiquette (see e.g. 562–4, where the monsters are depicted in a *comitatus* of their own, with cannibal feasts at the bottom of the sea). Moreover, this parody can impinge on that which it parodies—we hear of Grendel's 'guð-cræft' (127) and although he is clearly not an admirable warrior like Scyld or Hrothgar he 'rixode' (144) in Heorot, during the night, as not only Hrothgar but God allowed him to. The fact that he acts with God's permission is made quite clear (e.g. 478f., 705–9). Against the efforts of men to build a civilization—one aspect of which is a historical understanding—is pitted an irrational principle of instinctive animus, built in to the world by its Maker and, in a complex way, historical too (Cain was not a legendary figure, we suppose, for the poet or his audience).

Notes

Work on this essay was facilitated by a short period of study at Christ Church, Oxford, in the summer of 1992. I am most grateful to the College for its hospitality. All quotations from *Beowulf* refer to the edition by C.L. Wrenn, revised by W.F. Bolton (3rd ed., revised, Exeter, 1988). Diacritics have been omitted. Where quotations are not displayed, the break between half-lines is indicated by a vertical line thus: |

1. Nuttall, 'Virgil and Shakespeare', and Medcalf, 'Virgil at the Turn of Time', in *Virgil and his Influence: Bimillenial Studies*, ed. Charles Martindale (Bristol, 1984.), pp. 76, 239. Dr Medcalf also kindly discussed his article with me.

2. Michael Hunter, 'Germanic and Roman Antiquity and the Sense of the Past in Anglo-Saxon England', *Anglo-Saxon England* 3 (1974), pp. 46–8.

3. Adelaide Hardy, 'Historical Perspective and the *Beowulf* Poet', *Neophilologus* 63 (1979), pp. 431, 441. For a more positive view, Roberta Frank, 'The *Beowulf* Poet's Sense of History', in *The Wisdom of Poetry*, ed. Siegfried Wenzel and Larry D. Benson (Kalamazoo, 1982), pp. 53–65. I have not been able to see Leonard Tennenhouse, '*Beowulf* and the Sense of History', *Bucknell Review* 19 (1971), 137–46.

4. '*Beowulf* the Monsters and the Critics', *Proceedings of the British Academy* 22 (1936): separate publication, p. 5.

5. See, for instance, Olga Fischer, 'A Comparative Study of Philosophical Terms in the Alfredian and Chaucerian Boethius', *Neophilologus* 6 (1979), 622–39, and Jerold C. Frakes, *The Fate of Fortune in the Early Middle Ages: the Boethian Tradition* (Leiden, 1988). I owe the latter reference to Dr Clare A. Lees.

6. W.F. Bolton, 'Boethius and a Topos in *Beowulf*,' in Margot H. King and Wesley M. Stevens eds, *Saints Scholars and Heroes: Studies in Medieval Culture in Honour of Charles W. Jones* (Minnesota, 1979), vol. 1, p. 36.

7. Ruth Morse, *Truth and Convention in the Middle Ages: Rhetoric, Representation, and Reality* (Cambridge, 1991), pp. 95, 87.

8. J. Leyerle, 'The Interlace Structure of *Beowulf*', *University of Toronto Quarterly* 37 (1967), 1–17.

9. Tolkien, *op. cit.*, p. 29.

10. Sisam, *The Structure of 'Beowulf'* (Oxford, 1965), p. 22: Bolton, *ed. cit.*, p. 76.

11. See *The Seafarer*, ed. Ida L. Gordon (1960), p. 8; *The Wanderer*, ed. T.P. Dunning and A.I. Bliss (1969), p. 82; W.A. Camps, *An Introduction to Virgil's 'Aeneid'* (Oxford, 1969), pp. 54–8.

12. I take heart from the splendidly sceptical essay by E.C. Stanley, 'The Date of *Beowulf*: some Doubts and no Conclusions', in Colin Chase, ed., *The Dating of 'Beowulf'* (Toronto, 1981), pp. 197–211, reprinted in Stanley's *A Collection of Papers with Emphasis on Old English Literature* (Toronto, 1987). We can date the *manuscript* of the poem c. 1000 and its language is West Saxon with some Anglian elements: all else is conjecture.

13. For some stylistic comments on the handling of time see Håkan Ringbom, *Studies in the Narrative Technique of 'Beowulf' and Lawman's 'Brut'* (Åbo, 1968), pp. 25–37 (a not entirely reliable study, however), and E.G. Stanley, 'The Narrative Art of *Beowulf*', in *Medieval Narrative: a Symposium*, ed. Hans Bekker-Nielsen *et al.* (Odense, 1979), pp. 59f.

14. Stanley, 'Narrative Art'. p. 76.

THOMAS A. PRENDERGAST ON MEMORY AND THE IDOLATROUS PLEASURES OF HEROIC POETRY

Pleasure, at least earthly pleasure, was seen as a distraction from the pleasure that one was to take in God. Certainly this kind of concern led the fifth-century monk, John Cassian, to lament that his didactic, divine meditations were giving way to more seductive, secular images: "my mind is filled with those songs of the poets so that even at the hour of prayer it is thinking about those trifling fables, and the stories of battles with which from its earliest infancy it was stored by its childish lessons: and when singing Psalms or asking forgiveness of sins either some wanton recollection of the poems intrudes itself or the images of heroes fighting presents itself before the eyes, and an imagination of such phantoms is always tricking me and does not suffer my soul to aspire to an insight into things above."[8] These images that distract him from meditations on the divine were so troubling and offensive to early ecclesiastics that patristic psychology had categorized them as symptomatic of uncleanness (*immunditia*)—(as the Abbot Nesteros tells Cassian) a form of fornication.[9] Yet, like Augustine's more famous memories of the tears of Dido,[10] these seductive images of heroic poetry were often deemed necessary to help develop the memory (especially in children) precisely because they were so easily remembered.[11] What, then, facilitated the remembrance of scriptures was also what might distract one from constructive memories. This is why reactions to heroic poetry in the Anglo-Saxon period are characterized by a mixture of attraction and horror. Given this ancient acknowledgment of and bias against the seductive powers of heroic poetry,[12] it is perhaps not surprising that at the poem's narrative threshold, the narrator should explicitly articulate the double bind of remembering the heroic past as at once cleansing and seductive; he suggests that whatever objections there might be to remembering the "former days," the poem's inscribed audience is apparently eager to hear tales about those days.[13] The problem confronting the poet, as Fred Robinson and others have pointed out, is to validate this desire to remember (and thus validate remembering the poem itself) without valorizing the kind of obsessive remembering that led to the disastrous cycle of vengeance which plagued the Anglo-Saxon world—a mnemonics that, in the poem, is enabled by the seductive idolatry of violence. The *Beowulf*-poet attempts to solve this cultural problem by distinguishing between two kinds of memory—an impure, compulsive, and idolatrous remembering that reinforces a self-destructive culture of revenge, and a conscious remembering that constructively remembers the past without, in the process, valorizing the compulsion of kinstrife. By invoking and then differentiating between these two paradigms of memory, the poet is able to justify his own remembering of the past; for encoded within the poem is a strategy for how to read it—a way to reform and purify even the memory of the pagan Germanic past. Yet the poet cannot escape the central paradox underlying his project: his attempts to cleanse memory lead him to memorialize the very seductions that led to "uncleanness."

The problems inherent in distinguishing between conscious and compulsive memory are initially expressed in Beowulf's inability to cleanse Heorot; for if his conscious "remembering of his own fame" enables him to rid the hall of literal monsters,[14] he cannot cleanse Heorot of the monstrous kinstrife that pollutes the Hall because its inhabitants compulsively remember and hence reenact past injuries.[15] The poet offers some insight into just how difficult it is to sanitize memories when, in one of the more notorious passages of the work, the Danes offer sacrifices to idols. These idle supplications lead the poet (in a somewhat unusual authorial intrusion) to lament the "hope of the heathens" ("hæþenra hyht"), who, because they did not know of Heaven, "remembered Hell" ("helle gemundon") (l. 179). Using the verb "to remember" for the first time here, the poet meditates on the more problematic side of memory; for by remembering Hell the Danes can only return compulsively to a past custom that, the audience knew, perpetuated rather than eliminated evil.

The narrator's condemnation of hellish remembering is, of course, characteristically Christian in its disclosure of how futile it is to try to destroy evil by participating in a kind of compulsive and idolatrous remembering. But it also says much about the cultural connection between aesthetics and memory, for this Christian way of thinking about idolatry relies on troping memory as an inscribed image. Augustine—perhaps *the* medieval authority on memory—claimed that those who worshipped idols objectified their experience of the deity: they remembered the deity as an idolatrous object in order to assert mastery over him.[16] Hence they read the sign, which points "to an absence or a significance yet to come," as the thing itself.[17] John Freccero has argued that this kind of misreading has much to do with Augustine's famous definition of sin as enjoying that which should be used (27). This "enjoyment" is illicit because all things should ultimately point toward the deity. Thus, to enjoy the sign for its own sake is to fetishize the sign at the expense of the deity. From this perspective one might read the *Beowulf*-poet's characterization of the idols that the Danes worshipped as fetishes, as "a desperate attempt to render *presence*, a reified sign" that ultimately points to nothing (28). The root of this misreading becomes clear when the poet writes that the Danes "remembered Hell." They compulsively locate meaning in the physical sign (that is, the idols). As one of the points of the poem is that the Danes are unable to control remembering, the narrator's exclamation, "they did not know how to worship" ("herian ne cuþon") (l. 182), suggests that it was the misguided attempt to control the absent deity via mnemonic representations that led them, ironically, to extend the hellish violence of Grendel.

Nowhere is this pathology of idolatry more apparent than in the interstice between the death of Grendel and his metonymic reappearance via his mother. The idolatrous nature of this interstice is emblematized by Grendel's severed arm which Beowulf enshrines inside the hall. The arm is supposedly, as the poem says, a "clear sign" ("tacen sweotol") that Beowulf had "remedied all the grief" ("ealle gebette inwidsorge")—a mnemonics that purportedly leads to the cleansing of the past; yet, given the bloody events that follow, it seems, instead, that the arm is a *tacen* that uncleanness now lies at the heart of Heorot (ll. 825–36).[18] Rather than point beyond itself to a conscious transcendence of violence, the arm becomes a kind of fetish object that makes manifest an idolatrous worship of violence. Indeed, Grendel's severed arm becomes a kind of tourist attraction, as the poem tells us that people came from near and far "to look on the wonderful thing" ("wundor sceawian") (l. 840). At this particular moment in the poem, this "sign" seems to signal the triumph of heroic force over hellish force. Yet the Danes are quickly disabused of this latter notion when the kin of Cain once again makes its appearance in the hall. This multiplication of monsters seems to suggest that eliminating Grendel's mother will not cleanse the hall either. The impurity remains within Heorot (that is, within those who are within Heorot); for the poem hints that even if the kin of Cain are dead, the sin for which Cain was proscribed will be reenacted by Hrothgar's nephew.[19]

Certainly, this connection between violence, idolatry, and compulsion is reinforced by the apparent relish with which the poet describes the evisceration and consumption of Beowulf's erstwhile friend Hondscioh:

Ne þæt se aglæca yldan þohte,
ac he gefeng hraðe   forman siðe
slæpende rinc,   slat unwearnum,
bat banlocan,   blod edrum dranc,
synsnædum swealh;   sona hæfde
unlyfigendes   eal gefeormod,
fet ond folma.
          (ll. 739–45)[20]

[Nor thought the monster long to delay that, but, at the first occasion, he quickly seized a sleeping man, tore without hindrance, bit bonelocks, drank blood in streams, swallowed in huge morsels, at once he had consumed the lifeless one, feet, hands and all.]

The poet's tendency to dwell, with rhetorical excess, on the fragmentation of the body may be said to titillate the reader with evocative images of disembowelment—hence normalizing a kind of sadistic pleasure.[21] Georges Bataille has argued that such conflicting impulses of revulsion and fascination in the face of murder are primary: that is, the very idea that murder is transgressive inspires in the spectator (or reader) a kind of erotic frisson.[22] Yet if the reader is implicated in a kind of textual fornication here, it is because the reader or auditor is interpellated into the position of Beowulf himself as she or he follows the eroticized description of the death of the "slæpende rinc"; for, as the narrator tells us immediately prior to Grendel's gruesome bloodsport, "The exceedingly strong one watched . . . how the wicked ravager . . . would proceed" ("þryðswyð beheold . . . hu se manscaða . . . gefaran wolde") (ll. 736–38). The poet, here, erases all distinction between audience and fictional character, and thus implicates the audience more closely in Beowulf's idolatrous and voyeuristic gaze. The pleasure derived from this idolatry is, arguably, akin to the fetishistic pleasure associated with the *blazon*, which, as Roland

Barthes has demonstrated, destroys or dismembers the body in an effort to remember it idolatrously. The fragmentation of Hondscioh's body into "hands and feet," then, becomes a desperate attempt to render presence that leads only to a compulsive pleasure in destruction.[23]

Notes

8. John Cassian, *The Works of John Cassian*, tr. Rev. Edgar C. S. Gibson, vol. 11, The Nicene and Post-Nicene Fathers, 2nd ser., ser. eds. Philip Schaft and Henry Wace (Grand Rapids, Mich., 1983), p. 441.

9. Some time earlier, Augustine had explicitly laid out how the soul, "having found its delight in those corporeal former movements, since it cannot have them with it within itself, . . . becomes entangled with their images which it has fixed in its memory, and is foully defiled by the fornication of the fantasy; and it refers all its functions toward those ends for which it curiously seeks corporeal and temporal things through the senses of the body." Here, as in Cassian, the soul is portrayed as having a kind of adulterous intercourse with idle corporeal images, an obsessive interaction that prevents the soul from contemplating God; for the memory, where these images were stored, was seen as a storehouse in which the most vivid memories were associated with inner seeing (Augustine, *The Trinity*, tr. Stephen McKenna [Washington, D.C., 1963], p. 356).

10. Augustine, *The Confessions of St. Augustine*, tr. John K. Ryan (Garden City, N.J., 1960), p. 56.

11. For a brief discussion of "sex and violence" as at once something to be avoided and a "necessary component of the art of memory" in the later Middle Ages, see Mary Carruthers, *The Book of Memory* (Cambridge, 1990), p. 137.

12. As Fred Robinson has demonstrated, this particular tradition can be traced through Ælfric and Wulfstan (Fred Robinson, *"Beowulf" and the Appositive Style* [Knoxville, Tenn., 1985], pp. 8–9).

13. Robinson has suggested that the first line of the poem hints at the eagerness of the poet's historical audience to learn about pagan heroic deeds because *"gefrunon* (we have inquired) is a bolder word than . . . *gehyrdon* (we have heard) when considered in the context of ecclesiastical condemnation of those who" are curious about "songs about the pagan heroes of the *geardagum*" (Robinson, *"Beowulf" and the Appositive Style*, p. 89). As might be apparent, I tend to see the audience's eagerness as a construct of the poet rather than a reflection of a historical circumstance.

14. *Beowulf and the Fight at Finnsburg*, ed. Fr. Klaeber (Lexington, Mass., 1950), l. 659; hereafter cited in text by line number. Translations, unless otherwise noted, are mine.

15. The obsessive-compulsive nature of sin is biblical. See Prov. 26:11–13 and 2 Pet. 2:2.

16. Augustine, *On Christian Doctrine*, tr. D.W. Robertson Jr. (New York, 1954), p. 85.

17. John Freccero, "The Fig Tree and the Laurel: Petrarch's Poetics," *Literary Theory/Renaissance Texts*, ed. Patricia Parker and David Quint (Baltimore, 1986), p. 27; hereafter cited in text.

18. Perhaps more problematic from an ideological point of view is Grendel's mother. Here the social norms affirmed by the poem are at odds with the ethical ideals that the poet offers in his intermittent critique of the heroic code; for the attack by Grendel's mother exemplifies at once "monstrous" repetition *and* kin-loyalty. Her vengeance, according to the heroic code, is justified. Yet, despite the monster-woman's loyalty to her kin, the poet does not present Grendel's mother as a laudatory example of the heroic code; rather she is, like her son, a monstrosity who deserves it when the sword "broke her bonerings" ("banhringas bræc") and cut completely through her bodily flesh (ll. 1567–68).

19. For a brief discussion of Hrothulf's future treachery, see Howell D. Chickering Jr., *Beowulf* (New York, 1977), pp. 320–22.

20. As James Rosier wryly comments, "were the morsel not a thane, the process of eating might be that of any Anglo-Saxon gourmet" (James Rosier, "The Uses of Association: Hands and Feasts in *Beowulf*," *PMLA*, 78 [1963], 9). The thane, of course, is not named until Beowulf himself tells the tale.

21. Such drawn out imagistic representations of "death," André Bazin suggests, are "the negative equivalent of sexual pleasure" (André Bazin, *What is Cinema?*, tr. Hugh Gray [Berkeley, 1967–71], 2:173).

22. "The sight or thought of murder can give rise to a desire for sexual enjoyment . . . on the one hand the horror of death drives off . . . on the other an element at once solemn and terrifying fascinates us." See Georges Bataille, *Erotism: Death and Sensuality*, tr. Mary Dalwood (San Francisco, 1986), pp. 11–12, 45.

23. Roland Barthes, *S/Z* (Paris, 1970), pp. 120–21.

Bibliography

Abraham, Lenore. "The Decorum of *Beowulf.*" *Philological Quarterly* 72 (1993): 267–87.

Anderson, George K. *The Literature of the Anglo-Saxons.* 2nd ed. Princeton, NJ: Princeton University Press, 1966.

Anderson, Sarah. *Beowulf.* A Longman Culture Edition. New York: Longman, 2004.

Benson, Larry D. "The Originality of *Beowulf.*" *Harvard English Studies* 1 (1970): 1–43.

Berger, Harry Jr., and H. Marshall Leicester Jr. "Social Structure as Doom: The Limits of Heroism in *Beowulf.*" In *Old English Studies in Honour of John C. Pope*, ed. Robert B. Burlin and Edward B. Irving Jr. Toronto: University of Toronto Press, 1974, pp. 37–79.

Bloom, Harold, ed. *Beowulf.* New York: Chelsea House, 2007.

Bolton, Whitney F. *Alcuin and Beowulf: An Eighth-Century View.* New Brunswick, NJ: Rutgers University Press, 1978.

Bonjour, Adrien. *Twelve Beowulf Papers.* Geneva: Droz, 1962.

Cable, Thomas W. *The Meter and Melody of Beowulf.* Urbana: University of Illinois Press, 1974.

Chadwick, Nora K. "The Monsters and Beowulf." In *The Anglo-Saxons*, ed. Peter Clemoes. London: Bowes, 1959, pp. 171–203.

Chase, Colin, ed. *The Dating of Beowulf.* Toronto: University of Toronto Press, 1981.

Chickering, Howell. "Lyric Time in *Beowulf.*" *Journal of English and Germanic Philology* 91 (1992): 489–509.

Clark, George. *Beowulf.* Boston: Twayne, 1990.

Creed, Robert Payson. *Reconstructing the Rhythm of Beowulf.* Columbia: University of Missouri Press, 1990.

Damico, Helen, and John Leyerle, ed. *Heroic Poetry in the Anglo-Saxon Period.* Kalamazoo: Western Michigan University, 1993.

Desmond, Marilynn. "*Beowulf*: The Monsters and the Tradition." *Oral Tradition* 7 (1992): 258–83.

Donahue, Charles. "*Beowulf* and Christian Tradition: A Reconsideration from a Celtic Stance." *Traditio* 21 (1965): 55–146.

Foley, John Miles, and J. Chris Womack, ed. *De Gustibus: Essays for Alain Renoir*. New York: Garland, 1992.

Fulk, R.D., ed. *Interpretations of Beowulf: A Critical Anthology*. Bloomington: Indiana University Press, 1991.

Gardner, John C. "*Beowulf*." In Gardner's *The Construction of Christian Poetry in Old English*. Carbondale: Southern Illinois University Press, 1975, pp. 54–84.

Godfrey, Mary Flavia. "Beowulf and Judith: Thematizing Decapitation in Old English Poetry." *Texas Studies in Literature and Language* 35 (1993): 1–43.

Goldsmith, Margaret E. *The Mode and Meaning of Beowulf*. London: Athlone Press (University of London), 1970.

Greenfield, Stanley B. *Hero and Exile: The Art of Old English Poetry*. London: Hambledon Press, 1989.

Halverson, John. "The World of *Beowulf*." *ELH* 36 (1969): 593–608.

Hanning, Robert W. "*Beowulf* as Heroic History." *Mediaevalia et Humanistica* 5 (1974): 77–102.

Harris, Joseph. "Beowulf's Last Words." *Speculum* 67 (1992): 1–32.

Heaney, Seamus, trans. *Beowulf: A New Verse Translation*. New York: W. W. Norton, 2001.

Hill, John M. *The Cultural World of Beowulf*. Toronto: University of Toronto Press, 1995.

Howe, Nicholas. *Beowulf: A Prose Translation*. 2nd ed. Norton Critical Edition. New York: W. W. Norton, 2001.

Hume, Kathryn. "The Theme and Structure of *Beowulf*." *Studies in Philology* 72 (1975): 1–27.

Huppé, Bernard Felix. *The Hero in the Earthly City: A Reading of Beowulf*. Binghamton, NY: Medieval & Renaissance Texts Studies, 1984.

Irving, Edward B. Jr. *A Reading of Beowulf*. New Haven: Yale University Press, 1968.

———. *Rereading Beowulf*. Philadelphia: University of Pennsylvania Press, 1989.

John, Eric. "*Beowulf* and the Margins of Literacy." *Bulletin of the John Rylands Library* 56 (1974): 388–422.

Joy, Eileen A., and Mark K. Ramsey, and Bruce D. Gilchrist, eds. *The Postmodern Beowulf: A Critical Casebook*. Morgantown: West Virginia University Press, 2007.

Kendall, Calvin B. *The Metrical Grammar of Beowulf*. Cambridge: Cambridge University Press, 1991.

Kiernan, Kevin S. *Beowulf and the Beowulf Manuscript*. New Brunswick, NJ: Rutgers University Press, 1981.

McNamee, Maurice B. "Beowulf, a Christian Hero." In *McNamee's Honor and the Epic Hero*. New York: Henry Holt, 1960, pp. 86–117.

Mizuno, Tomoaki. "Beowulf as a Terrible Stranger." *Journal of Indo-European Studies* 17 (1989): 1–46.

Moorman, Charles. "The Essential Paganism of *Beowulf*." *Modern Language Quarterly* 28 (1967): 3–48.

Morgan, Gwendolyn A. "Mothers, Monsters, Maturation: Female Evil in *Beowulf*." *Journal of the Fantastic in the Arts* No. 13 (1991): 54–68.

Near, Michael R. "Anticipating Alienation: *Beowulf* and the Intrusion of Literacy." *PMLA* 108 (1993): 320–32.

Newton, Sam. *The Origins of Beowulf and the Pre-Viking Kingdom of East Anglia*. Cambridge: D. S. Brewer, 1993.

Nitzsche, Jane Chance. "The Structural Unity of *Beowulf*: The Problem of Grendel's Mother." *Texas Studies in Literature and Language* 22 (1980): 287–303.

Ogilvy, J. D. A., and Donald C. Baker. *Reading Beowulf*. Norman: University of Oklahoma Press, 1983.

Overling, Gillian R. *Language, Sign, and Gender in Beowulf*. Carbondale: Southern Illinois University Press, 1990.

Pearsall, Derek. "*Beowulf* and the Anglo–Saxon Poetic Tradition." In *Pearsall's Old English and Middle English Poetry*. London: Routledge & Kegan Paul, 1977, pp. 1–24.

Pope, John C. *The Rhythm of Beowulf*. New Haven: Yale University Press, 1966.

Robinson, Fred C. *Beowulf and the Appositive Style*. Knoxville: University of Tennessee Press, 1985.

———. *The Tomb of Beowulf and Other Essays on Old English*. Oxford: Basil Blackwell, 1993.

Schrader, Richard J. *Old English Poetry and the Genealogy of Events*. East Lansing, MI: Colleagues Press, 1993.

———. "Succession and Glory in *Beowulf*." *Journal of English and Germanic Philology* 90 (1991): 491–504.

Sorrell, Paul. "Oral Poetry and the World of *Beowulf*." *Oral Tradition* 7 (1992): 28–65.

Stitt, J. Michael. *Beowulf and the Bear's Son: Epic, Saga, and Fairytale in Northern Germanic Tradition*. New York: Garland, 1992.

Tolkien, J.R.R. *Beowulf and the Critics*. Tempe: Arizona Center for Medieval and Renaissance Studies, 2002.

Wormald, Patrick. "Bede, *Beowulf*, and the Conversion of the Anglo-Saxon Aristocracy." In *Bede and Anglo-Saxon England*, ed. Robert T. Farrell. Oxford: British Archaeological Reports, 1978, pp. 32–95.

Contributors

Harold Bloom is Sterling Professor of the Humanities at Yale University. He is the author of thirty books, including *Shelley's Mythmaking, The Visionary Company, Blake's Apocalypse, Yeats, A Map of Misreading, Kabbalah and Criticism, Agon: Toward a Theory of Revisionism, The American Religion, The Western Canon,* and *Omens of Millennium: The Gnosis of Angels, Dreams, and Resurrection. The Anxiety of Influence* sets forth Professor Bloom's provocative theory of the literary relationships between the great writers and their predecessors. His most recent books include *Shakespeare: The Invention of the Human,* a 1998 National Book Award finalist, *How to Read and Why, Genius: A Mosaic of One Hundred Exemplary Creative Minds, Hamlet: Poem Unlimited, Where Shall Wisdom Be Found?,* and *Jesus and Yahweh: The Names Divine.* In 1999 Professor Bloom received the prestigious American Academy of Arts and Letters Gold Medal for Criticism. He has also received the International Prize of Catalonia, the Alfonso Reyes Prize of Mexico, and the Hans Christian Andersen Bicentennial Prize of Denmark.

J.R.R. Tolkien, author of *The Hobbit* and *The Lord of the Rings,* was professor of Anglo-Saxon at Oxford University, where he established himself as a pre-eminent philologist and medievalist.

Joan Blomfield wrote extensively on medieval literature and was the author of "The Style and Structure of Beowulf."

Stanley B. Greenfield was a University of Oregon professor of English and an internationally recognized expert in Old English literature. His books include *A Critical History of Old English Literature, The Interpretation of Old English Poems, A Readable Beowulf,* and *A New Critical Study of Old English Literature.* He also received a Guggenheim Fellowship, a Fulbright Fellowship, and a senior fellowship from the National Endowment for the Humanities.

Edward B. Irving, Jr. was a professor of English at the University of Pennsylvania, specializing in medieval literature. Some of his works include *Reading Beowulf*, *An Introduction to Beowulf*, and *Rereading Beowulf*. He also coedited *Old English Studies in Honour of John C. Pope*.

T.A. Shippey is a scholar of medieval, particularly Anglo-Saxon, literature as well as of modern science fiction and fantasy. He teaches at Saint Louis University, where he is the Walter J. Ong Chair of Humanities, is the author of *The Road to Middle-Earth*, *J.R.R. Tolkien: Author of the Century*, and *Roots and Branches: Selected Papers on Tolkien*. He has also edited the anthologies *The Oxford Book of Fantasy Stories* and *The Oxford Book of Science Fiction Stories*.

James W. Earl is a professor of English at the University of Oregon and the author of *Thinking about Beowulf* and coeditor of *The World of Literature*.

David Williams is the author of *Cain and Beowulf: A Study in Secular Allegory*.

Linda Georgianna is the author of *The Solitary Self: Individuality in the Ancrene Wisse*.

Susanne Weil is a member of the department of English at Centralia College.

Paul Dean is the author of "Beowulf and the Passing of Time."

Thomas A. Prendergast is the coeditor of *Rewriting Chaucer: Culture, Authority, and the Idea of the Authentic Text: 1400–1602*.

Acknowledgments

Tolkien, J.R.R. "Beowulf: The Monsters and the Critics," Sir Israel Gollancz Memorial Lecture, proceedings of the British Academy, 1936.

Blomfield, Joan. "The Style and Structure of Beowulf," *The Review of English Studies*, Vol. 14, no. 56 (October 1938). Reprinted by permission of Oxford University Press.

Greenfield, Stanley B. "Geatish History: Poetic Art and Epic Quality," *Neophilologus*, 47 (1963). Reprinted with kind permission from Springer Science and Business Media.

Irving, Jr., Edward B. From *A Reading of Beowulf.* New Haven: Yale University Press, 1968.

Shippey, T.A. From *Beowulf.* Southhampton, England: Edward Arnold, 1978. Reprinted by permission of T.A. Shippey.

Earl, James W. "The Necessity of Evil in Beowulf," *South Atlantic Bulletin*, Vol. 44, no. 1 (January 1979). Used by permission.

Williams, David. *Cain and Beowulf: A Study in Secular Allegory*, University of Toronto Press, 1982. Reprinted by permission of University of Toronto Press.

Georgianna, Linda. "King Hrethel's Sorrow and the Limits of Heroic Action in Beowulf," *Speculum* 62 (1987): 829–834.

Weil, Susanne. "Grace Under Pressure: Hand-Words, Wyrd, and Free Will in Beowulf," *Pacific Coast Philology*, Vol. 24, no. 1/2 (November 1989). Used by permission.

Dean, Paul. "Beowulf and the Passing of Time: Part 1," *English Studies* 3, 1994. Reprinted by permission of Taylor and Francis Ltd., http://www.tandf.co.uk/journals

Prendergast, Thomas A. "Wanton Recollection": The Idolatrous Pleasures of Beowulf. *New Literary History* 30:1 (1999), 130–133, 139–141. © *New Literary History*, University of Virginia.

 Index

Character in literary works are indexed by first name (if any), followed by the name of the work in parentheses.